new beginnings

Scottish National Gallery
of Modern Art

new beginnings

postwar British art from the collection of **Ken Powell**

Alastair Grieve

Published on the occasion of the exhibition
New Beginnings: Postwar British Art from the Collection of Ken Powell
at the Scottish National Gallery of Modern Art, Edinburgh
13 November 1992 – 3 January 1993
Graves Art Gallery, Sheffield, 16 January – 13 March 1993
Published by the Trustees of the National Galleries of Scotland

ISBN 0 903598 28 0
Photography by Antonia Reeve and Tate Gallery (front cover)
Designed by Dalrymple
Typeset in Dante and Univers, both issued in 1957
Printed by Balding+Mansell

foreword

We owe a profound debt of gratitude to Ken Powell for agreeing to part with his works for as long as six months, thus making this exhibition, and its subsequent showing in Sheffield, possible. He has also welcomed us into his home on numerous occasions and willingly shared with us his knowledge of, and enthusiasm for, his collection. Grateful thanks are also due to Dr. Alastair Grieve, Senior Lecturer at the University of East Anglia, for his essay and catalogue entries which amount to an important contribution to the art literature of the period; and to Alice O'Connor for speedy and accurate typing of all the material at short notice.

Timothy Clifford
Director, National Galleries of Scotland

Richard Calvocoressi
Keeper, Scottish National Gallery of Modern Art

acknowledgements

This catalogue is dedicated to the memory of Adrian Heath who died on September 15th 1992. As well as being a marvellous and productive painter, Adrian was the most active of his circle during the fifties in organizing exhibitions and publications devoted to their abstract art. My essay is based on *Nine Abstract Artists* which is the best known of the many exhibitions for which he was responsible. Without his activities then we would have no context in which to study postwar British abstract art. He provided an essential focus.

Ken Powell gave vital information for the catalogue and made the task of writing it very enjoyable. He is as good a cook as he is a collector. Keith Hartley, Assistant Keeper of the Scottish National Gallery of Modern Art, added much necessary detail. Norma Carroll typed it efficiently and fast.

Alastair Grieve

introduction

The last few years have seen a renewed interest in British art (particularly abstract art) of the 1950s. The St. Ives 'school', the constructivists, those artists associated with the Independent Group, have all attracted the attention of historians and collectors alike, who recognised that their work represented a return by British art to the central concerns of International Modernism, an attempt to break away from the partly enforced, partly self-imposed parochialism of the War years. Neo-Romanticism seemed both inward- and backward-looking, whereas the pure lines of constructivism, for example, seemed in tune with the new progressive, optimistic mood of postwar Britain, a necessary adjunct to the New Towns and modern housing estates. Art could play its part in creating a new Britain.

Ken Powell's collection represents this aspect of postwar British art exceedingly well. Its main characteristics are a concentration on abstract and largely constructivist art and an unswerving insistence on quality. Powell has never hesitated to sell works in order to refine and improve his collection. Indeed, he has sold a whole collection in the past because he realised that he could not afford to buy the best works of their type.

He did not begin by collecting postwar British art. Indeed, in the 1950s he was buying Georgian glass and Chinese porcelain, an area he continued in until the early 1960s. He then sold his collection of Chinese porcelain and turned to collecting Camden Town paintings. Typically, it was an exhibition (at Agnew's) that attracted his attention and set him off in a new direction. He was able to build up a quite respectable group of Camden Town works but eventually realised that with rising prices he could no longer afford to buy top quality paintings by some of the artists. He therefore began to broaden out his collection of British art and to sell his Camden Town works. He bought works by Robert MacBryde, Winifred Nicholson, Christopher Wood and others. But it was in 1972 when he saw the exhibition *The Non-*

Objective World 1939-1955 at Annely Juda Fine Art that his interest in constructivist works was really kindled. He bought several works from this show. Annely Juda introduced him to several of the artists, such as Anthony Hill and Gillian Wise. Later he got to know Prunella Clough and Jack Smith through Monika Kinley. Gradually he became increasingly interested in this area. He deepened his knowledge by reading and looking at as much art of the period as he could. (Powell is a firm believer in the two cardinal rules of collecting: know your subject in depth and only buy the best.) He refined his collection by selling off all extraneous works and by selling or swapping in order to buy something major. For example, he swapped a Scott, a Hilton and an Ivon Hitchens for his large Lanyon painting *Longshore* (no.48).

For Powell one of the major pleasures of collecting postwar British abstract art has been the opportunity it afforded him of becoming friends with several of the artists. The annual parties to which he invites his artist friends and others from the art world, have become famous in their way: proof, if it were needed, that art is not a separate activity but part and parcel of life itself. Truly successful collecting is not an amassing of expensive items to decorate one's walls, but a willingness on the collector's part to integrate the art into his own life.

Keith Hartley
Assistant Keeper, Scottish National Gallery of Modern Art

Alastair Grieve

abstract art in Britain in the 1950s

Late in 1954 a small book was published titled *Nine Abstract Artists*. It was followed early in 1955 by an exhibition of the same name at the Redfern Gallery. The nine artists were Robert Adams, Terry Frost, Adrian Heath, Anthony Hill, Roger Hilton, Kenneth Martin, Mary Martin, Victor Pasmore and William Scott. These artists, all represented in Ken Powell's collection, were the most exciting of the younger generation of abstract artists working in Britain at that time and the book and accompanying exhibition are vital landmarks in the history of the period. The book consists of statements by each artist, reproductions of their work and an extremely informative introduction by the critic Lawrence Alloway who was invited to contribute by Adrian Heath, the main organiser of book and exhibition. Though the nine artists did not have a shared style, all agreed that, in abstract art, medium and meaning were bound together as never before and that the abstract work was an object in its own right, with positive forms and colours which affected the environment in which it was placed

Alloway divides the nine artists into two groups, a core of constructivists, consisting of Pasmore, Kenneth and Mary Martin, Heath, Hill and Adams, 'who pick up the intentions and character of *Circle*', the 1937 publication of constructive art edited by Ben Nicholson, Naum Gabo and J. L. Martin; and Frost, Hilton and Scott who 'represent the other extreme of non-figurative art – irrational expression by *malerisch* means.'[1] The two groups were not self-contained. Frost, especially, shared ideas with Pasmore and Heath who were based in London, even though he worked in the West Country, at St. Ives and Corsham, in art communities with whom Hilton and Scott also came to be associated and where the landscape and the figure remained important inspirations.

Pasmore showed his first abstract paintings in May 1948 with the London Group. These works were similar to his poster for the exhibition (no.62, colour plate p.32), which was revolutionary at the time. Its composition is not abstracted from nature but built up from basic shapes, triangle, circle, square, which rotate in linked turns down and across the rectangular format. Pasmore was influenced partly by Paul Klee and partly by theoreticians of harmonious proportion such as J. W. Power, Matila Ghyka, Jay Hambidge and Le Corbusier, whose books (listed in the bibliography p.64) were circulating in his group. He used their diagrammatic explanations of the golden section, the moving format, root rectangles and so on, to replace the effects of natural beauty, such as twilight or mist on the Thames, that he had exploited so successfully in immediately preceding paintings. The extreme hostility aroused by his conversion to constructed abstract art led him and his fellow converts to organise their own exhibitions and publications of which *Nine Abstract Artists* is the best example.

Kenneth Martin, who taught with Pasmore at Camberwell School of Art, abandoned flat depictions of North London scenes, less picturesque than those Pasmore had painted (e.g. no.49), and showed his first abstract paintings in 1950. Mary Martin did likewise. Heath, prompted by Pasmore, showed a small abstract painting inspired by Power's explanation of the moving format at the London Group in December 1949 but did not commit himself fully to abstract art until 1951 when he was active in organizing a group exhibition, *Abstract Painting, Sculptures, Mobiles*, at the A.I.A. Gallery. Adams, who started to teach in 1949 with Pasmore at the Central School of Art under the enlightened principal William Johnstone, did not convert suddenly. He was the only sculptor in the group and he contributed to their exhibitions radically abstracted figures, of wood, stone or metal rod, built up of basic forms, which he had been developing since 1947. His prints, probably made at the Central School, have similar abstracted figures (e.g. no.1). Hill, who studied at the Central School with Adams and Pasmore, was exceptional in not being trained in an academic, figurative tradition. By 1950 he was constructing abstract collages built up of basic forms with a restricted colour range (nos.35 and 36, colour illustration on back cover).

Collage is used by all the constructivists in Powell's collection, either in its own right or as a preliminary to paintings. Paper or card is cut into basic shapes which are built up to suggest movement and organic growth. Another important source book for their method was D'Arcy Thompson's *On Growth and Form*, which demonstrated the mathematical laws underlying the development of nature's forms through time. This helped them to produce art which was not abstracted from the appearance of nature but which used her structural processes.

The paintings and prints by Adrian Heath and Kenneth Martin in Powell's collection (nos.31 and 50-52), are good examples of this constructive building. Similar works are reproduced in their first publication devoted to their new art and ideas, *Broadsheet No.1*, which they issued in conjunction with their exhibition at the A.I.A. in 1951. Here Kenneth Martin wrote:

> *The abstract painting is the result of a creative process exactly the opposite to abstraction ...*
> *Proportion and analogy are at the base of such a pictorial architecture. The painting grows according to these laws and these have their counterpart in the laws of nature. Not painting which imitates the illusory and transient aspects of nature, but which copies nature in the laws of its activities.*[2]

Heath's painting (no.31, colour plate p.27) was shown at the A.I.A. exhibition and reproduced in *Nine Abstract Artists* where he wrote of his method of building up forms, derived from sub-divisions of a particular rectangular format, worked out first in collage.

> *It is the process, the method of development that is the life of the painting, and this that absorbs my interest rather than the attractions of any particular form or colour. The forms themselves, their size and position are born from the process. In fact all forms should witness clearly to their evolution. The colour and shape of their past is responsible for their present which is richer for these transitions.*[3]

After the exhibition at the A.I.A. in the summer of 1951 there were further shows with the London Group and in 1952-53 Heath organised more exclusive exhibitions of their art in his studio at 22 Fitzroy Street, off the Tottenham Court Road, which laid the foundations for the more ambitious exhibition *Nine Abstract Artists*.[4] Starting with the London Group show of November 1951 there was a move by some of the painters into more 'concrete' three-dimensional art forms so that the space in later exhibitions was animated by mobiles and constructed reliefs as well as collages, paintings and sculptures. Kenneth

Martin developed logically from abstract painting to mobiles of proportionally related rectangles of painted tin hung from dowel rods and then, in 1953, to screw mobiles of standard stock brass brazed in rhythmic sequence onto a vertical steel rod. His wife Mary, inspired partly by Le Corbusier's *Modulor*, moved from painting to shallow reliefs in which cubes and half cubes are marshalled in climbing, spiralling sequences between clearly defined foreground and background planes (nos.54 and 55). She used only white or grey believing that colour was too emotive and had naturalistic associations.

Other artists in the group also severely restricted their range of colour. Pasmore's last *Spiral* paintings, his collages and his early constructed reliefs, are mostly black and white with accents of maroon and ochre. Hill, too, restricted himself to black and white and the positive, flat colours of industrial paints (nos.37 and 38).

An interest in industrial materials and techniques developed logically from their abandonment of traditional painting. They were encouraged in this direction by the American constructionist Charles Biederman whose great book *Art as the Evolution of Visual Knowledge* (1948) they read and with whom some of them carried out lengthy correspondences.[5] Biederman argued that the last contribution to the long tradition of artists' attempts to interpret nature in paint had been made by Mondrian in c.1917. The next step, which Biederman himself put into practice, was the relief constructed from modern materials such as plastic sheet and coloured aluminium. Pasmore exhibited his first reliefs made from such materials in their exhibitions in 1952, to the further dismay of his earlier patrons, and by the summer of 1954 had developed the type of which Powell's is an example (no.63). Pre-cut laths of plywood are grouped vertically, in subtle asymmetric formation, on either side of a central spine. Further subtleties of depth and light and shadow are formed by the plane of transparent plastic, above and below which the grouped vertical planes float and which unites them with the surrounding space.

Pasmore's brave example was followed by Anthony Hill who developed his first reliefs alongside his last black and white geometric paintings in the mid-fifties. Powell's marvellous *Orthogonal Composition* of 1954 (no.38) is Hill's most recent painting reproduced in the book *Nine Abstract Artists*, while in the exhibition with the same title held in January 1955 he showed his first relief, a horizontal progression of black and white plastic rectangles.[6] Both clearly related to the kind of abstract art pioneered by Mondrian, van Doesburg, Gabo, Max Bill and others which Hill describes in his statement in the book as:

> *an art for a new age, a non-mimetic art aiming at an aesthetic of objective invention and sensation, distinctly rational and determinist in contrast to the subjectivist limbo in which the greater part of art is today submerged.*[7]

In subsequent reliefs Hill perhaps exploits the qualities of industrial materials more deliberately than Pasmore (nos.39 and 40). He uses planes of aluminium angle, clear, tinted and opaque plastic sheet, which he juxtaposes in rhythmic, asymmetric groups. His control of tone, surface texture and space is astonishingly sophisticated.

While moving from painting into relief constructions, Hill was joined by John Ernest, an American artist who had settled in London in 1951. With Pasmore's encouragement Ernest too abandoned painting and in 1955 made his first small relief with a composition of vertical planes arranged on the golden section.[8] In subsequent, more ambitious reliefs (eg. no.27) he used machine-driven tools to create sequences of immaculately crafted planes of modern sheet materials. Ernest delights in, yet manages to control, the variety of surfaces industry has given us and he plays off, for example, buffed stainless steel against glossy vinyl or matt, teak-faced plywood.

A yet more adventurous use of the colours of machine-made materials, as well as the introduction of light into the heart of the relief by means of prisms, is found in the relief by Gillian Wise (no.71) She met Hill in the summer of 1958 through Charles Biederman with whom they were both corresponding, and in 1963 they shared an exhibition at the Institute of Contemporary Arts. No.72 is a joint work shown in that exhibition.

Because of their use of industrial materials and their move into real space, Pasmore and the group around him collaborated enthusiastically with architects. From 1955 Pasmore himself was involved in designing the south-west area of Peterlee New Town and in the following year all members of the group contributed to the important environmental exhibition *This is Tomorrow* at the Whitechapel Art Gallery. John Ernest's small construction in Powell's collection (no.26) is a maquette for one of two towers he showed there in a pavilion he designed with Anthony Hill.

Here, as well as free-standing constructions, they showed their first reliefs and replicas of works by pioneer Russian abstract artists such as Malevich. All were made of modern sheet materials. In the following year Mary Martin and Adams designed monumental architectural reliefs for a new hospital in Belfast and a new theatre in Gelsenkirchen, Germany, respectively, and Pasmore, with Richard Hamilton, constructed a walk-through *Exhibit* of suspended acrylic panels at the Hatton Gallery, Newcastle-upon-Tyne. Their architectural activities reached a climax in 1961 in the temporary buildings erected for the Congress of the International Union of Architects on the South Bank to which Adams, Hill, Kenneth and Mary Martin, Gillian Wise and John Ernest contributed very large wall reliefs, mobiles, a constructed tower and free-standing sculpture.

Their concern with relating their art to the new architecture was shared by the ex-COBRA artist Stephen Gilbert as is shown by his *Construction with Aluminium Plates* of 1954 (no.30). In the year he made it, he showed a maquette for a kiosk, of coloured metal planes, at an exhibition organised by the group at the London Building Centre to demonstrate how the machine could be used creatively. Though British, Gilbert lived in Paris and so did not play a major part in the group's other activities. He was, however, an important link with developments on the Continent, introducing them, for example, to the Dutch ex-COBRA artist Constant Nieuwenhuys, who was also moving from painting into architectural constructions, and arranging for the French critic R.V. Gindertael to write about their work in the influential magazine *Art d'Aujourd'hui*.[9] Gilbert himself was a member of the Paris-based *Groupe Espace* who, strongly influenced by the inter-war ideas of Rietveld and van Doesburg, believed in a total integration of architecture, painting and sculpture by means of coloured planes arranged orthogonally. Gilbert's *Construction with Aluminium Plates* of 1954 was followed, in 1955-57, by ambitious projects for a house and flats of coloured metal and glass.[10]

The English constructivists were not exclusive, as is shown by their inclusion in *Nine Abstract Artists* and in some of their other early exhibitions of Frost, Hilton and Scott – the artists described by Alloway as representing 'the other extreme of non-figurative art – irrational expression by *malerisch* means.' Frost, when studying with an ex-serviceman's grant at Camberwell School of Art in the late forties, had been introduced by Pasmore and his colleagues to theories of harmonious proportion. His first surviving abstract painting, of 1949, relates to Pasmore's early abstracts and to those by Heath and Kenneth Martin discussed above, but in subsequent paintings Frost succeeds in incorporating within his compositions of linked circular and rectangular shapes suggestions of the movement of boats along the harbour wall at St. Ives where he lived.[11] Later, in 1954-6 when holding a Gregory Fellowship at Leeds University, the stone walls and fields of Yorkshire found their way into his paintings. Powell's *Pink Quay* of 1956 (no.28, colour plate p.26) shows a fusion of forms derived from Frost's London friends and the environments of Cornwall and Yorkshire.

Hilton's painting titled *February-March 1954* (no.42, colour illustration on front cover) is one of five dated that year which he exhibited in *Nine Abstract Artists*. It is also reproduced in the book where Hilton remarks in his accompanying statement:

> *I suppose few artists really know what they are doing; it is an instinctive, irrational, activity.*[12]

Though this statement seems to place him in confrontation with the artists producing constructed, geometric art, discussed above, he shared with them an avoidance of illusory space. His statement goes on to describe his liking for strongly contrasted, dynamic colours which activate the environment in which the picture is placed. Hilton had developed these fine paintings, with their dense, opaque surfaces, primary colours and black, on white grounds, after studying the works of Mondrian on a visit to Holland with Constant in February 1953. From Holland they had gone on to visit Gilbert in Paris where they all contributed lithographs to a folio organized by Gilbert. Nos.29 and 41 come from this folio and bear witness to the increasing architectural structure in their work which emerged, in Hilton's case, from Paris-based *tachisme* and in Gilbert's and Constant's from the expressionism of COBRA. Though Hilton was at his most abstract at the time of *Nine Abstract Artists*, faint suggestions of the figure can be detected in his pictures shown then and these become stronger in subsequent works. He considered working with Adams on a pavilion at *This is Tomorrow* but did not, in fact, exhibit again with them. He spent the Christmas of 1956 with Heron in Cornwall, which he visited frequently in the following years, introducing allusions to the landscape as well as the figure into his paintings from 1957.

Scott, too, is associated with Cornwall, which he visited regularly from 1946. Though he was producing his most austere abstract paintings, with emphatic rectilinear black lines knifed into dense, white, heavily painted surfaces, at the time of *Nine Abstract Artists* and even from a year or two earlier he always retained a suggestion of the figure, often ambiguously interchangeable with table-top still life or harbour scene. His paintings also suggest sophisticated comments on the traditions of primitive and naïve painting of which he was aware from teaching in Brittany and from the pictures of Alfred Wallis. Scott wrote in *Nine Abstract Artists*:

> *I am an abstract artist in the sense that I abstract. I cannot be called non-figurative while I am still interested in the modern magic of space, primitive sex forms, the sensual and erotic, disconcerting contours, the things of life.*[13]

There are other artists from West Cornwall in Powell's collection whose work was not sufficiently abstract for *Nine Abstract Artists*, Lanyon and Heron among them. Lanyon, born in St. Ives in 1918, was influenced by Nicholson and Gabo in 1939 but after the war sought inspiration in his own Cornish roots, tin-mining and fishing. The veins of red in Powell's two gouaches of 1952 (nos.43 and 44) can be seen as ore in a mine, though the forms also have erotic, sexual connotations. Lanyon saw the relationship of sea to land on the Cornish north coast as male to female. His association with Scott and the sculptor Kenneth Armitage at Bath Academy of Art, Corsham, where he taught from 1952-7 and where he drew the fine *Nude* (no.46), must have reinforced his interest in a fusion between the human body and the landscape. Lanyon connected the shapes, textures and colours of his painting with physical activity such as climbing or gliding which he took up in 1959. He said:

> *I paint the weather and high places and the places where solids and fluids meet. The junction of sea and cliff, wind and cliff, the human body and places all contribute to this concern.*[14]

Longshore (no.48, colour plate p.29), Powell's largest and latest Lanyon, painted two years before the artist's untimely death in a gliding accident in 1964, is an exhilaratingly gusty recreation in paint of the sea and wind against the shore.

Patrick Heron's paintings until the mid-fifties are figurative and reflect his admiration for Braque and Matisse. Then, in 1956, following his move to a house with an established, exotic, wild garden at Zennor near St. Ives, he produced a series of canvases with loose, overlapping, rectangular brushmarks and vibrant runs of paint evoking blossom and seasonal change. These seem to show a switch in allegiance on Heron's part from the *École de Paris* to American artists, such as Sam Francis and Bradley Walker Tomlin. They were shown in the spring of the following year in an exhibition at the Redfern Gallery titled *Metavisual Tachiste Abstract* which was devoted largely to gestural painters and where two constructed reliefs by Pasmore must have seemed out of place.

Heron followed his garden paintings in 1957-8 with a remarkable series of stripe paintings and in 1958-9 he introduced uneven, soft-edged rectangles and circles of colour onto all-over colour fields (see no.34, colour plate p.28). Again, these paintings inevitably raise the question of the influence of American painting, in this case of Rothko in particular, a problematic question which there is not space to enter into here.[15]

Powell's collection also has significant works by artists who were active at the time *Nine Abstract Artists* was published but whose aims were different from those in the book. By the winter of 1954 something of a rivalry had developed between Pasmore's circle and another, formed under the wing of the Institute of Contemporary Arts in 1952, which we have come to know, since c.1962, as the Independent Group.[16] To begin with, at least, the two groups were not mutually exclusive. Pasmore and Hill, for example, attended some meetings organized by the I.G., while Turnbull and Paolozzi, members of the I.G. well represented in Powell's collection, were included in some of the early abstract exhibitions. Both groups drew inspiration from Klee, Moholy-Nagy and D'Arcy Thompson's *On Growth and Form*.

After studying at the Slade together, Turnbull and Paolozzi had gone to Paris in the late forties where they were profoundly influenced by the art of Picasso, Giacometti, Richier, Dubuffet and the collections and ideas of the Dadaist Tzara and the Surrealist Breton. Some of this is evident in their works in Powell's collection (nos.56,58,59,60,68 and 69). Evident, too, is their fascination with the time-battered 'existentialist' individual, exemplified especially in their renditions of the human head. Paolozzi's bronze *Mannikin* (no.61) is similar to works he showed at *This is Tomorrow* in a pavilion, planned with Nigel Henderson and the architects Alison and Peter Smithson, in which the scattered shards of former civilizations suggested a bleak, Beckett-like, terminal existence.

Not at all evident in the art they exhibited at the time, is their counterbalancing fascination with the alluring, consumer culture of the U.S.A., which seemed to postwar Europeans like a Golden Age of the immediate future. The bellboy in Paolozzi's *Collage* (no.57) calls us to wonder at the uplifting cornucopia of American goodies which both awaken our desires and promise their fulfilment. Paolozzi's famous *Bunk* lecture, given at the Institute of Contemporary Arts in spring 1952, when he projected, in rapid succession, pages torn from American science fiction magazines and pulp advertisements, must have punched home a similar message, though in a less structured form.

Even further from the ideals of the nine abstract artists in the fifties are Jack Smith and Prunella Clough who are also both well represented in Powell's collection. Smith had shown realist paintings at the Beaux Arts Gallery from 1952 and in 1956 was one of the group of so-called 'kitchen sink' artists in the British section at the Venice Biennale. His pictures of this time, painted in cold greys and browns, are of easily read domestic scenes. In *Figures and Objects in a Room* of 1959 (no.66) he has developed a subtler range of tones and an excitingly fluid, Cubist space. His large *Light Movement* of 1962 (no.67) recalls the Futurist Balla's abstract painting of coloured light while acknowledging a more sophisticated technology. Yellow and pale reds interpenetrate with blue and deeper red to suggest pulsating waves of light.

Clough was not one of the realists who showed at the Beaux Arts Gallery but her work, from c.1945 to c.1955, is powerfully representational. Her drawing of *Man Filleting Fish* (no.10) and her oil of *Printer Cleaning Press* (no.17, colour plate p.25) capture, in an unsentimental and committed way, the responsibility and dignity of manual labour. Her muted colours and method of composing, the way, for example, she incorporates the printer within the insistent geometry of his working environment, accords with the lives of her subjects. On the other hand, her series of *Drawings for Modelling Stand* (nos.12,13 and 14) seem to show an awareness of the complex space and poetic, studio subjects of Braque's late works, while in her monotypes and etchings her respect for Klee is apparent (nos.20-24). Her graphic work here has a sense of exactness coupled with ambiguity. She seems to have abstracted the essence of subjects but left them veiled to the viewer.

The decade of the fifties closed with a flourish for many of the artists in Powell's collection. Clough had a retrospective exhibition at the Whitechapel Art Gallery in 1960. In the same year the constructivists showed in Zurich in a major international exhibition of *Konkrete Kunst* organized by Max Bill. Pasmore had a one-man exhibition at the Venice Biennale. In the following year they contributed largely to the I.U.A. Congress, as mentioned above, and they organized an exhibition at the Drian Gallery, London, which brought together their work of the previous decade. Of course, at the same time, the artistic climate was changing. Caro exhibited one of his first coloured welded steel sculptures at the same I.U.A. Congress. The *Situation* exhibition at the R.B.A. Galleries in September 1960 brought out a group of young painters also strongly indebted to large-scale American colour field painting. At the *Young Contemporaries* exhibition at the same gallery in the following year, Hockney and his fellow graduates from the Royal College paraded their first Pop paintings. After 1960 avant-garde art seems to have been accepted more easily by a wider public than in the fifties. It was perhaps because they were so isolated, so much dependent on themselves, that the artists of the fifties seem so exciting.

notes

1 L. Alloway, *Nine Abstract Artists, their Work and Theory*, London 1954, p.3.

2 K. Martin, *Abstract Art, Broadsheet No.1, Devoted to Abstract Art*, published in conjunction with an exhibition of abstract art at the A.I.A. Gallery, 15 Lisle Street, W.C.2 from May 22nd to June 11th 1951.

3 *Nine Abstract Artists*, p.26.

4 See A. I. Grieve, 'Towards an art of environment: exhibitions and publications by a group of avant-garde abstract artists in London 1951-55', *The Burlington Magazine* CXXXII, no.1052, November 1990, pp.773-781 for a discussion of their exhibitions.

5 See A. I. Grieve, 'Charles Biederman and the English Constructionists', *The Burlington Magazine* CXXIV, No.954, September 1982, pp.540-551 and CXXVI, No.971, February 1984, pp.67-77.

6 *Anthony Hill, Retrospective Exhibition*, Hayward Gallery May-July 1983, no.20.

7 *Nine Abstract Artists*, p.28.

8 *John Ernest Constructions 1955-64*, Institute of Contemporary Arts, London 1 July – 1 August 1964, no. 1

9 R. V. Gindertael, 'Peintres Britanniques d'Aujourd'hui', *Art d'Aujourd'hui*, Série 4, no.2, March 1953, pp.12-15.

10 In collaboration with the builder Peter Stead of Huddersfield, Gilbert designed and constructed a model house early in 1955 but split with Stead in 1957 after making models for a cluster of 12-storey blocks of flats. Stead went on to build a house at Branch Lane, Almondbury, Yorkshire, adopting Gilbert's ideas. See *Architectural Design XXIX*, July 1959, pp.275-279.

11 *Terry Frost, Paintings, drawings and collages*, Arts Council / South West Arts 1976-77, no.6.

12 *Nine Abstract Artists*, p.29.

13 *Nine Abstract Artists*, p.37.

14 A. Causey, *Peter Lanyon*, Henley-on-Thames 1971, p.11.

15 Heron himself has written about it. See 'The Ascendancy of London in the '60's', *Studio International* Vol.172, no.884, December 1966, pp.280-281; 'A Kind of Cultural Imperialism?', *Studio International* Vol.175, no.897, February 1968, pp.62-64; 'The British Influence on New York', *The Guardian*, October 10, 11, 12, 1974. See also A. Bowness, 'An American Invasion and the British Response', *Studio International* Vol. 173, no.890, June 1967, pp.285-293 and A. Bowness, 'Introduction', *Patrick Heron, Recent Paintings*, The Whitechapel Art Gallery 21 June-16 July 1972.

16 See G. J. Whitham, *The Independent Group at the I.C.A. : Its Origins, Development and Influence 1951-1961*, Ph.D., University of Kent 1986, pp.391-392 and A. Massey and P. Sparke, 'The Myth of the Independent Group', *Block* 10, 1985, pp.48-56.

colour plates

Prunella Clough **Printer Cleaning Press** 1953 no.17

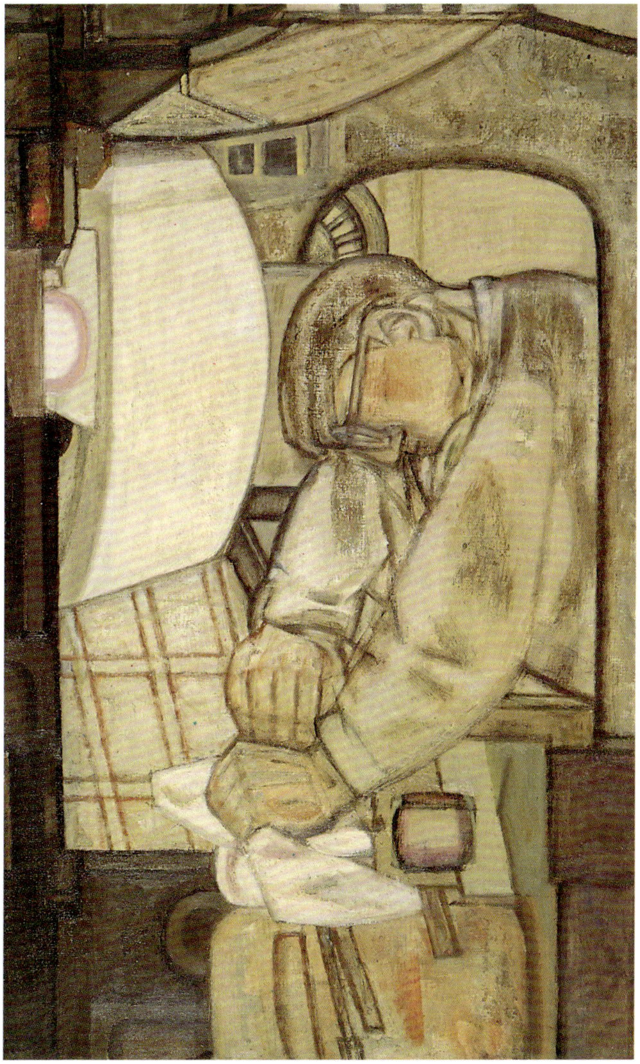

Terry Frost **Pink Quay** 1956 no.28

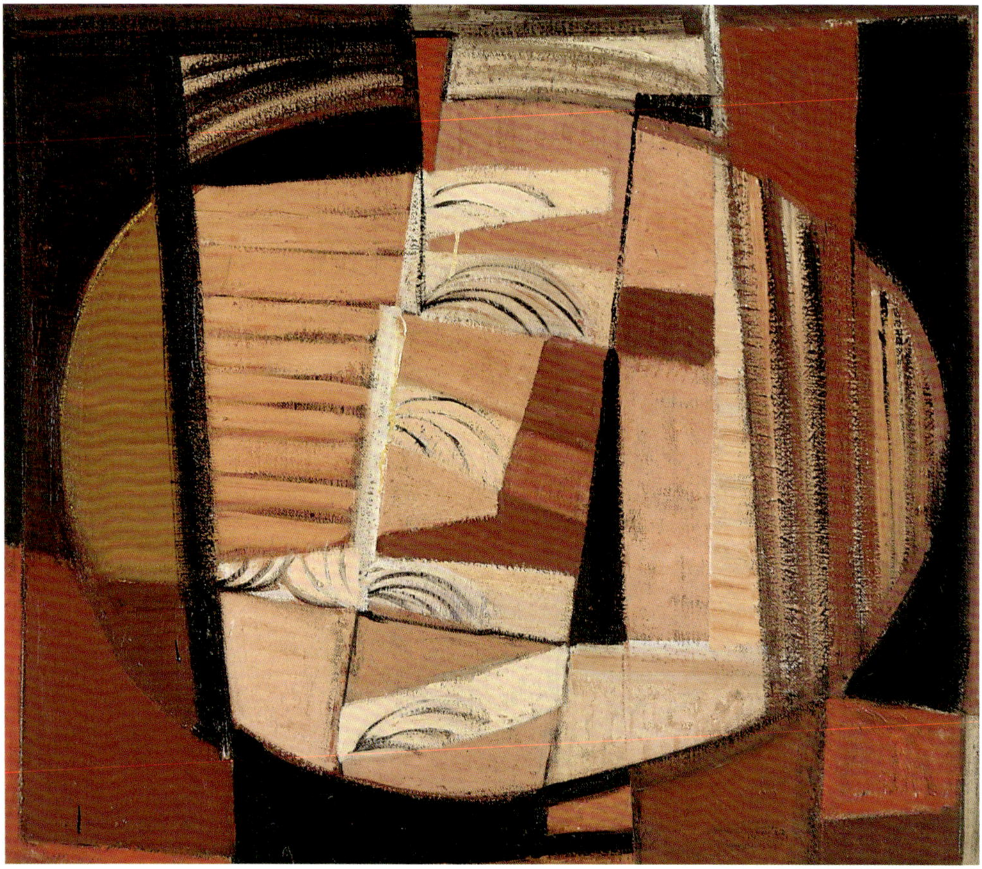

Adrian Heath **Climbing Composition Green and Blue** 1950 no.31

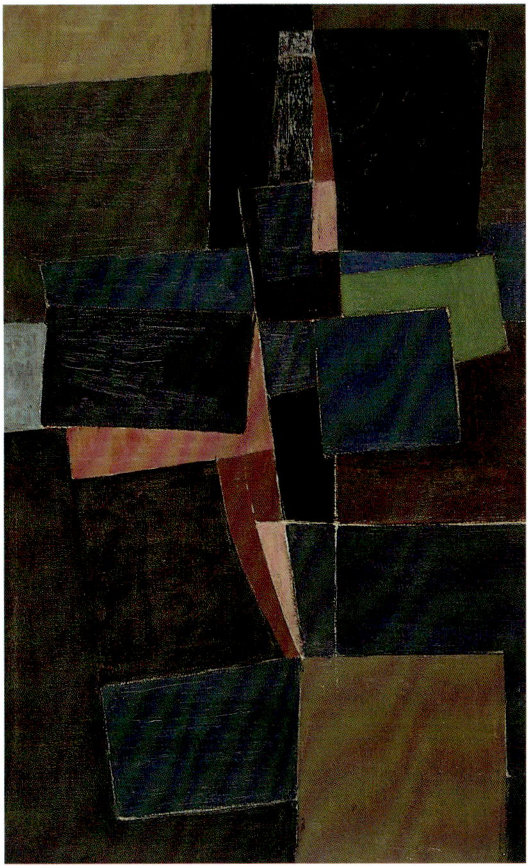

Patrick Heron **Blue Painting (Squares and Disc)** 1958-9 no.34

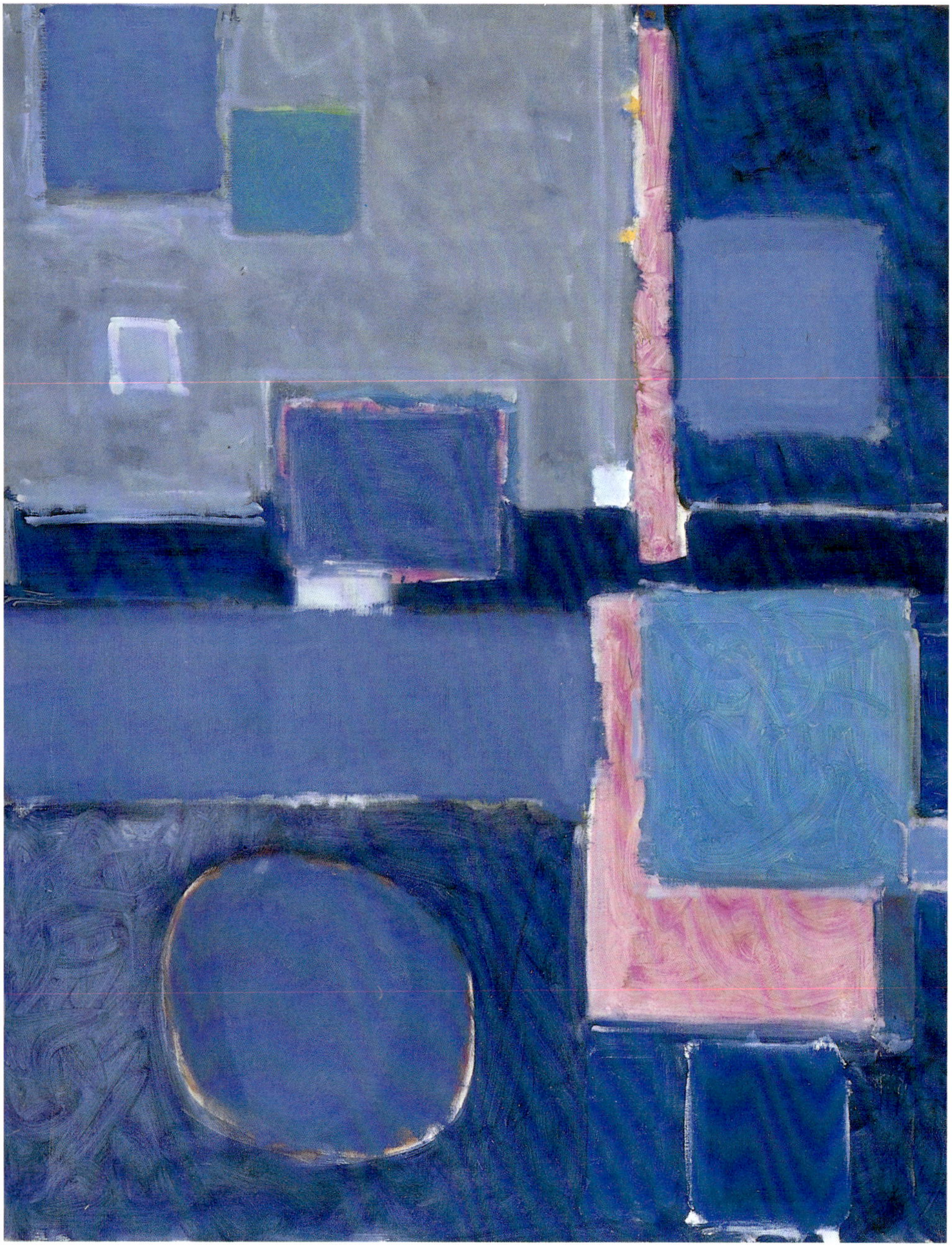

opposite Peter Lanyon **Longshore** 1962 no.48

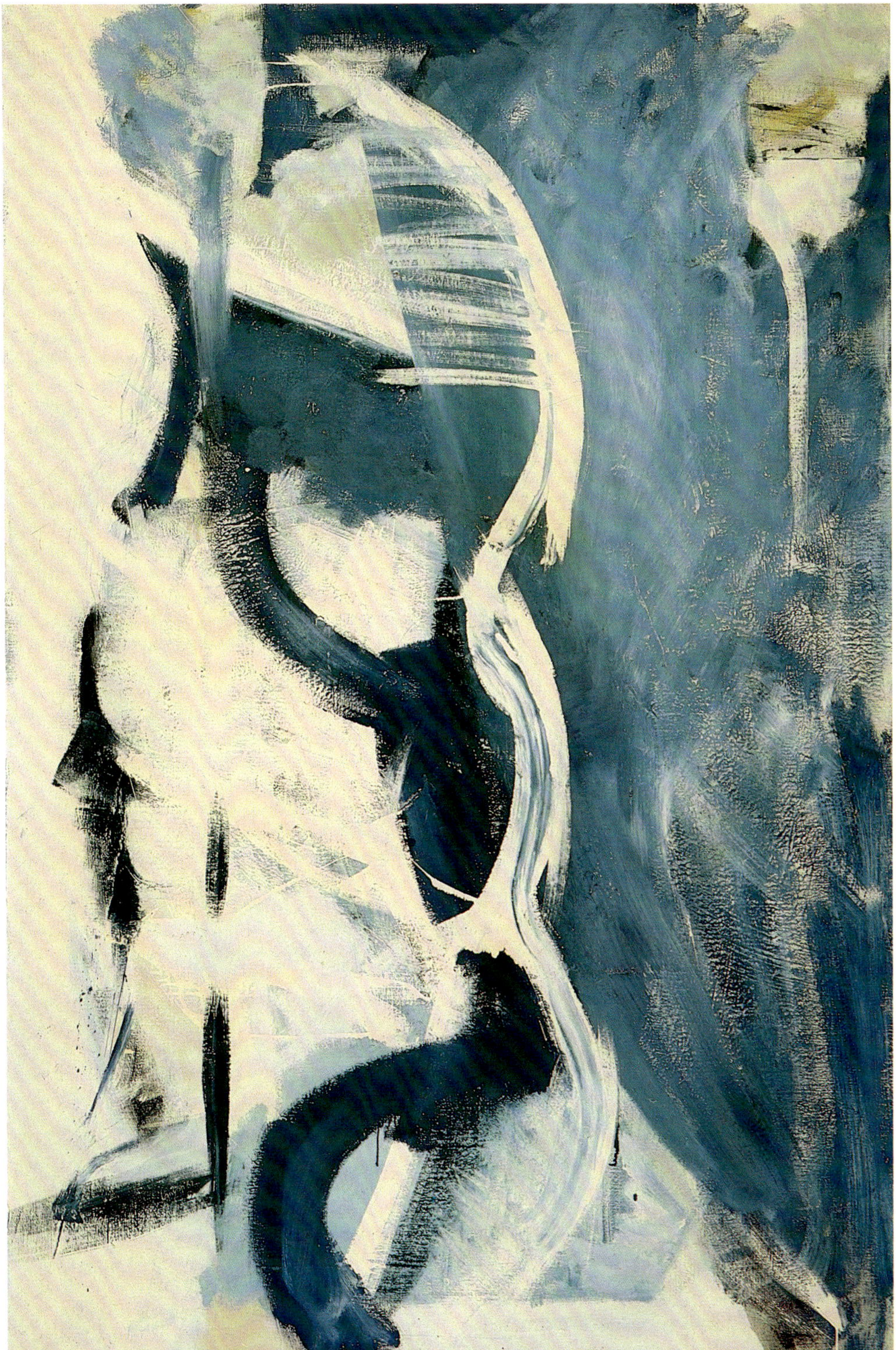

Kenneth Martin **Composition** 1949-50 no.50

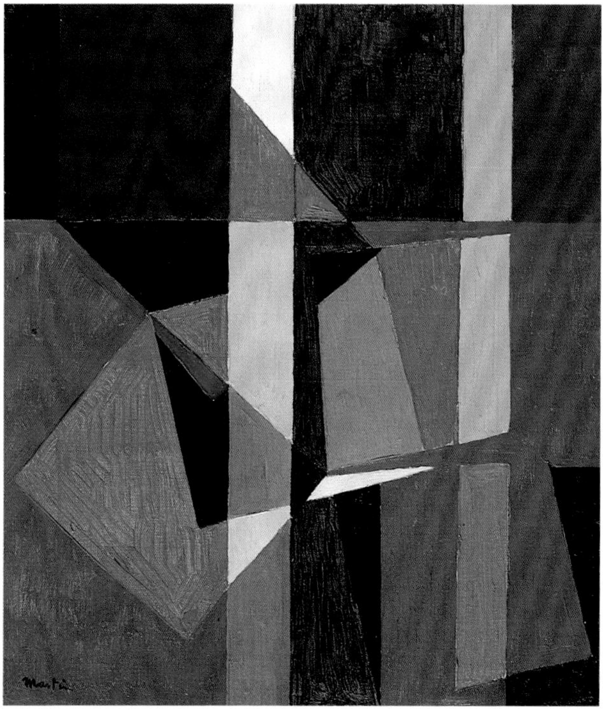

Eduardo Paolozzi **Collage** 1951 no.59

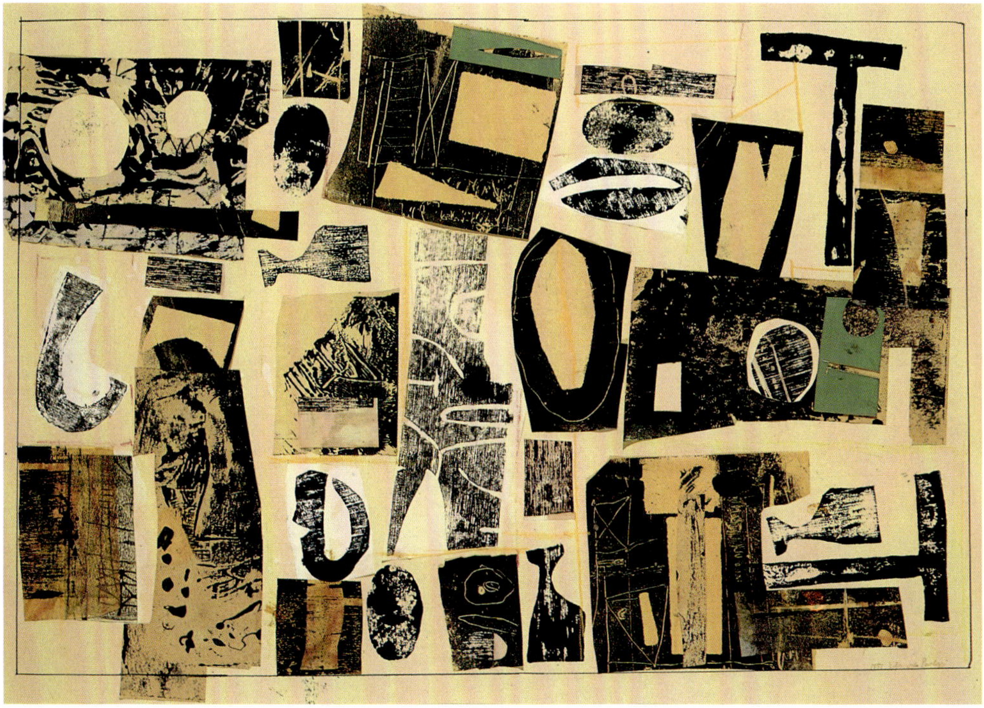

Victor Pasmore **Poster for London Group** 1948 no.62

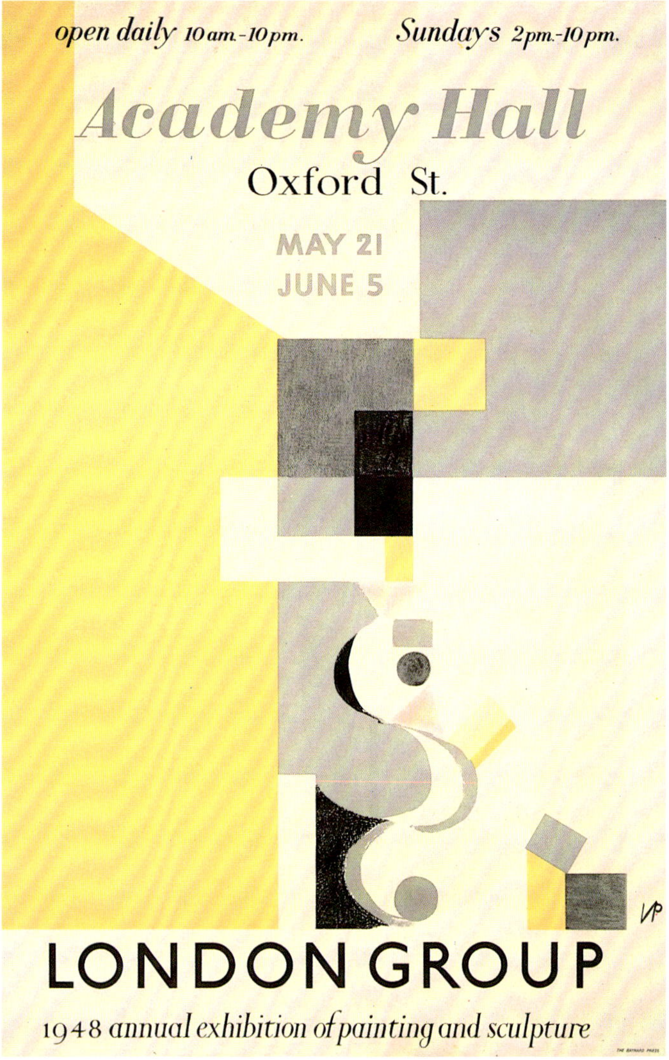

catalogue

Dimensions are in centimetres, height before width

In the case of prints, exhibition details do not necessarily refer to the particular impression in this collection

A short artist's bibliography is appended at the end of each entry

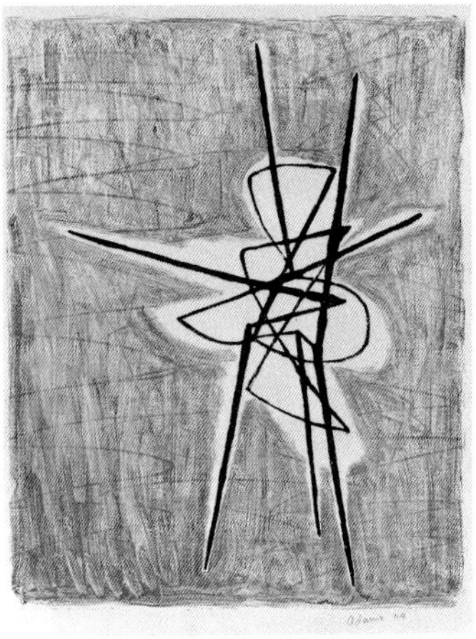

1

ROBERT ADAMS 1917-1984

1 **Untitled** (Standing Abstract Figure) 1949

Inscribed b.r.: 'Adams 49'
Lithograph with monotype colouring 26 × 28.5 cm (image size)
Lithograph not editioned
Purchased: William Weston Gallery, London 1987

Adams had his first one-man exhibition at Gimpel Fils Gallery, London in 1947-8 and he continued to show there regularly. From 1949 he taught at the Central School, London with Victor Pasmore and became a leading member of the group of abstract artists gathered around him. In 1951 Adams showed at the Festival of Britain and in 1952 with other young British sculptors at the XXVI Venice Biennale. Until 1956 he worked mainly in wood but in that year he turned to welded metal. He showed again at Venice in 1962. His last works, from 1970, are mainly in bronze.

Adams seems to have started to make prints at the Central School, where the master printer Ernest Devenish worked, and in 1949-50 made over a dozen lithographs and monotypes. In 1951 Adams won a prize for lithography at the I. Bienal, São Paulo.

This print resembles Adams's sculptures, of the same date, of abstracted figures constructed from brass or wood rods.

F. Carey and A. Griffiths, *Avant-Garde British Printmaking 1914-1960*, British Museum 1990
A. I. Grieve, *The Sculpture of Robert Adams*, Lund Humphries and the Henry Moore Foundation 1992
A. I. Grieve, *A Sculptor's Record*, Tate Gallery 1992

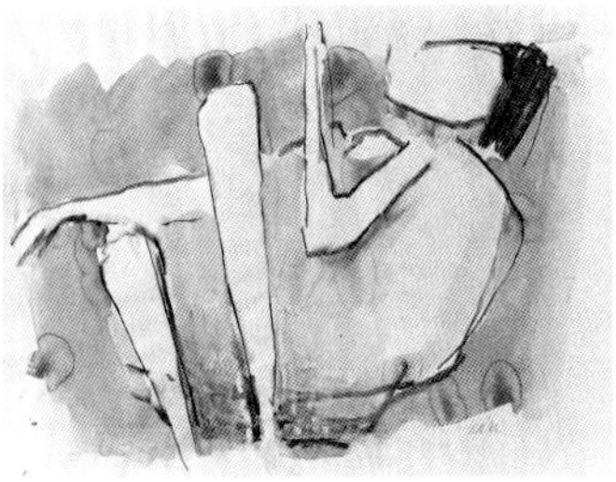

2

KENNETH ARMITAGE b.1916

2 **Untitled** (Reclining Nude) 1962

Inscribed l.r.: 'KA '62'
Charcoal and watercolour on paper 55.6 × 75.8 cm (paper size)
Purchased: New Art Centre 1990; ex. collection of Lilian Somerville

Like many leading 20th century British sculptors, Armitage was born in Yorkshire. He studied at Leeds College of Art 1943-7 and the Slade School, London 1937-9. From 1946-56, concurrently with William Scott, he taught at the Bath Academy of Art at Corsham. He was one of the group of young British sculptors who received international acclaim at the Venice Biennale of 1952. He had his first one-man exhibition at Gimpel Fils Gallery, London in the same year, held a Gregory Fellowship in Leeds 1953-5 and showed again at Venice in 1958 with Scott and S. W. Hayter, when he won the David E. Bright Award. Early on he carved stone but soon turned to modelling in plaster which he filed and chipped so that his bronze casts have the appearance of wall surfaces. Heads and limbs of immured, abstracted figures project from flat planes.

This fine drawing shows Armitage's planer modelling, with the figure's torso forming a background wall in front of which the limbs project in a parallel plane. It has much in common with the compositions of his colleague Scott.

N. Lynton, *Kenneth Armitage*, London 1962
S. Nairne and N. Serota, *British Sculpture in the Twentieth Century*, Whitechapel Art Gallery, London 1981
Kenneth Armitage, Retrospective Exhibition, Arts Council of Great Britain 1972-3
Kenneth Armitage, *Sculptures et Dessins, 1948-1984*, Artcurial, Paris 1985

3

GILLIAN AYRES b.1930

3 **Green, Orange, Black and White** 1956

Inscribed b.r.: 'Gillian Ayres 56'
Lithograph 55.8 × 40.5 cm (image size)
Exhibited: Redfern Gallery, London 1956-7, no.401; *British Prints, The Post-War Years, 1945-60*, Redfern Gallery January-February 1986, no. 10 (illus. in colour); *Avant-Garde British Printmaking 1914-1960*, British Museum September 1990-January 1991, no.219 (illus. in colour)
Purchased: Redfern Gallery, London 1986

Gillian Ayres studied at Camberwell School of Art from 1946-1950. She had her first one-person exhibition at Gallery One, London in 1956 and in the following year had 15 paintings included in the *Metavisual Tachiste Abstract* exhibition at the Redfern Gallery. In 1960 she exhibited in the *Situation* exhibition of large abstract paintings. She started to exhibit at the Kasmin Gallery, London in 1965. In 1977 she was represented in *British Art 1952-77* at the Royal Academy and in 1981 she had a one-person exhibition at the Museum of Modern Art, Oxford. She was elected ARA in 1982 and had a retrospective exhibition at the Serpentine Gallery in the following year which was toured by the Arts Council. She taught part-time at Corsham from 1959-1966, at St. Martins 1966-78 and was Head of Painting at Winchester from 1978-81.

From her earliest works Ayres has shown a delight in the texture of paint freely brushed onto white canvas and in the interaction of colour for its own sake. She shares this delight with Hilton while she also seems to have been influenced early on by Abstract Expressionist paintings by Robert Motherwell, Franz Kline and Clyfford Still which she may have seen at the exhibition *Modern Art in the United States* at the Tate Gallery at the start of 1956.

This lithograph was made at an evening class in lithography taught by Alistair Grant at Hammersmith. (See *Avant-Garde British Printmaking*, British Museum, pp.228-229)

Catalogues of exhibitions at Museum of Modern Art, Oxford 1981; the Serpentine Gallery, London 1983; the Arnolfini Gallery, Bristol 1989; Fischer Fine Art, London 1990
F. Carey and A. Griffiths, *Avant-Garde British Printmaking 1914-1960*, British Museum 1990

WILHELMINA BARNS-GRAHAM b.1912

4 **Untitled** 1958

Inscribed b.l.: 'W. Barns Graham 1958'
Lithograph 51.3 × 64.2 cm (paper size)
Not editioned
Purchased: New Art Centre, London 1986

Wilhelmina Barns-Graham studied at the Edinburgh College of Art from 1932-7. She moved to St. Ives in 1940 where she still works for part of the year, though, since 1973, she has spent increasing amounts of time near her native St. Andrews. Her numerous one-person exhibitions began at Downing's Bookshop, St. Ives, in 1947. In 1989 a major retrospective exhibition started in Newlyn and toured through Scotland. Among her many group shows are the *Crypt Group*, St. Ives 1947; *Abstract Painting, Sculptures, Mobiles*, A. I. A. Gallery, London 1951; *St. Ives 1939-1964*, Tate Gallery 1985.

Barns-Graham, like Ben Nicholson and many other St. Ives artists of the generation she met when she arrived there at the outbreak of the War, has abstracted geometric forms from the surrounding landscape and reconstructed them in paintings which are objects in their own right. Visits to glaciers in Switzerland in 1948 had a profound influence on her work and, more recently, she has been inspired by travel to Italy, Spain and the Orkneys. She uses abstract colours and forms to suggest movement, the transition of one state of being to another.

This lithograph is probably one of a group made by St. Ives artists with the help of the professional lithographic printer Stanley Jones. According to F. Carey and A. Griffiths, Jones set up a temporary lithography workshop in St. Ives in 1958 at the suggestion of Robert Erskine of the St. George's Gallery, London. (See *Avant-Garde British Printmaking 1914-1960*, p.179.) In this print the influence of Hans Hartung is evident. A similar influence can be seen in some of Robert Adams's drawings of the same period, when he and Barns-Graham were friends.

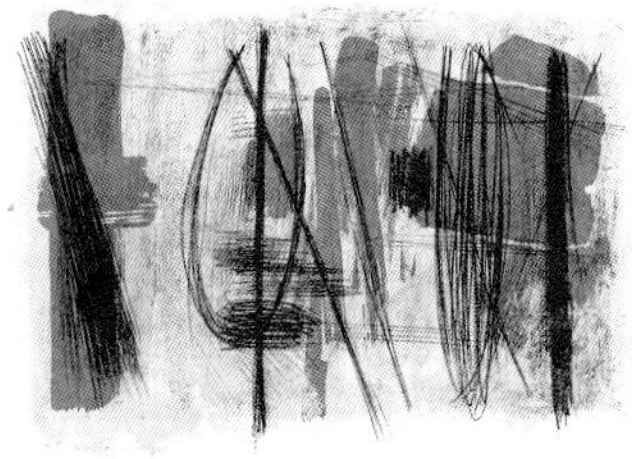

4

St. Ives 1939-64, Tate Gallery 1985
W. Barns-Graham, Paintings and Drawings, Crawford Centre for the Arts, St. Andrews 1982
W. Barns-Graham, Retrospective 1940-1989, City of Edinburgh Museums & Art Galleries 1989

REG BUTLER 1913-1981

5 **Archaic Head** 1952

Lead bronze 26.5 cm long
Exhibited: *Reg Butler*, Hanover Gallery, London April-June 1954, no.7; *Reg Butler*, Tate Gallery November 1983-January 1984, no.46
Purchased: Phillips, London 5 November 1991, no.78

Butler was a practising architect before the War. During it, he was a conscientious objector and worked as a village blacksmith. Afterwards, though he returned to architecture, he spent more and more of his time on sculpture. In 1948 he made his first work in forged iron and in July of the following year he was able to show an impressive group of linear sculptures in that material at the Hanover Gallery, London. From 1950 to 1953 he held the first Gregory Fellowship in sculpture at Leeds University which freed him for the time from financial constraints and enabled him to produce a series of major works. For the Festival of Britain in 1951 he made *Girl and Boy* . In 1952, using shell bronze, he made *The Oracle* on commission for Hatfield Technical College. In the following year his submission to the international competiton for a monument to 'The Unknown Political Prisoner' won the Grand Prize of £4,500.

Inquisitive, upward pointing heads are important in all these works. *Archaic Head* (no.5) resembles, particularly, the strange phallus-conning tower head which rears up from *The Oracle*, though parallels may also be drawn with the heads of the female watchers at the base of the scaffold-tower in the monument to 'The Unknown Political Prisoner'. Richard Calvocoressi has compared *Archaic Head* with tribal art from the Cameroons. (*Butler*, Tate Gallery 1983, p.20.) Ideas may also have come from Giacometti, such as his *Disagreeable Object* of 1932 and even Tod Browning's shocking film *Freaks*, also of 1932, in which one of the actors, 'Larva man', is all head.

The previous owner of *Archaic Head* was Robert Melville who wrote eloquently on Butler's sculpture as early as January 1952. ('The New Sculptors', *Harper's Bazaar*, January 1952, pp.33-5 and p.73.)

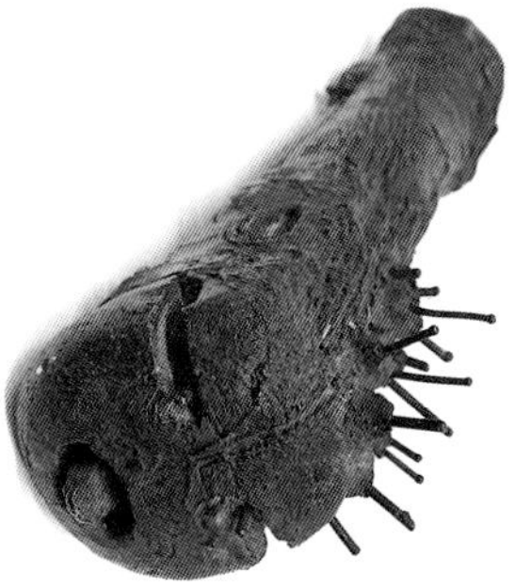

5

Reg Butler, Tate Gallery 1983
R. Burstow, 'Butler's Competition for a Monument to "The Unknown Political Prisoner" : Abstraction and Cold War Politics', *Art History*, Vol.12, no.4, December 1989, pp.472-496

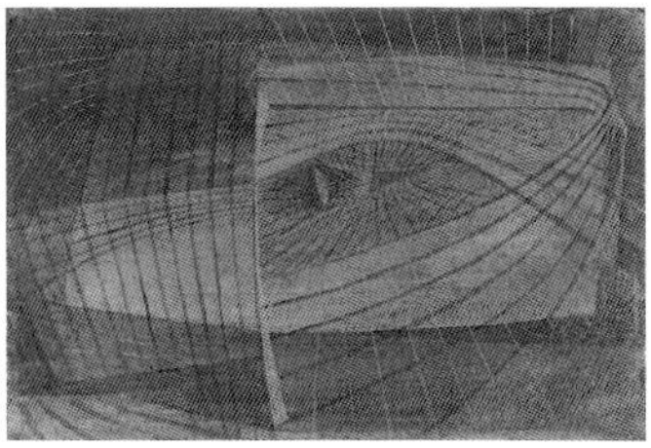

6

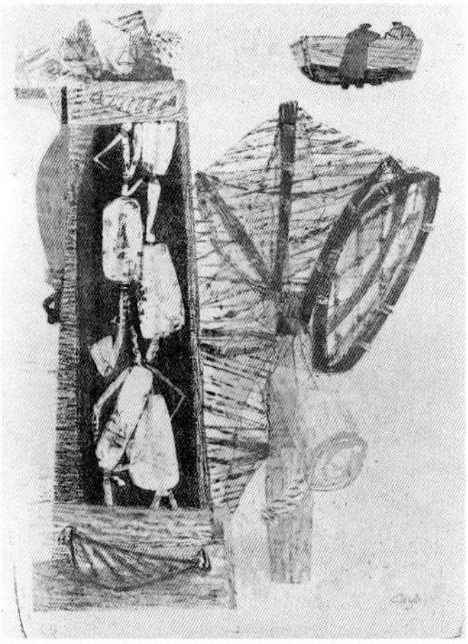

8

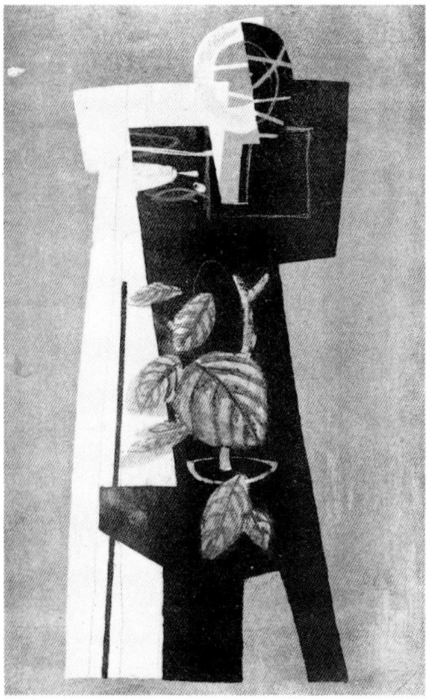

11

PRUNELLA CLOUGH b.1919

6 **Labyrinth** 1945

Inscribed b.r.: 'Clough'
Tempera on wood 25.2 × 38.1 cm
Purchased: The artist

7 **Still Life with Pears** 1948

Inscribed b.l.: 'Artist's proof' and b.r.: 'Clough'
Lithograph 15.1 × 20.2 cm (image size)
Exhibited: *Colour-Prints by the Society of London Painter-Printers*, Redfern Gallery, London November-December 1948, no.40
Purchased: Redfern Gallery, London 1975

8 **Eel-Net** 1948

Inscribed b.r.: 'Clough'
Lithograph 42.1 × 30.6 cm (paper size)
Exhibited: *Colour-Prints by the Society of London Painter-Printers*, Redfern Gallery November-December 1948, no.38; *British Prints, The Post-War Years, 1945-60*, Redfern Gallery January-February 1986, no.21; *Avant-Garde British Printmaking 1914-1960*, British Museum September 1990-January 1991, no.154
Purchased: Redfern Gallery, London 1975

9 **Plants in a Greenhouse** 1949

Inscribed b.l.: '2/15' (twice) and b.r.: 'Clough'
Lithograph 46.2 × 30.3 cm (paper size)
Exhibited: *Les Peintres-Graveurs*, Redfern Gallery December 1949, no.251; *British Prints, The Post-War Years, 1945-60*, Redfern Gallery January-February 1986, no.22
Purchased: Redfern Gallery, London 1975

10 **Man Filleting Fish** 1949

Inscribed b.r.: 'Clough'
Lithograph 38 × 28.3 cm (paper size)
Purchased: Redfern Gallery, London 1987

11 **Still Life on Modelling Stand** 1951

Inscribed b.r.: 'Clough' and t.c.: 'Proof'
Lithograph with chalk additions 38.3 × 24 cm (image size)
Not editioned; one of only 3-5 proofs
Exhibited: *Recent Colour Prints by the Society of London Painter-Printers*, Redfern Gallery December 1950-January 1951, no.222; *British Prints, The Post-War Years, 1945-60*, Redfern Gallery January-February 1986, no.23
Purchased: Redfern Gallery, London 1986

12 **Drawing for 'Still Life on Modelling Stand'** 1951

Gouache, pencil and chalk on card 35.3 × 21.2 cm (card size)
Given by the artist in the 1980s

13 **Drawing for 'Still Life on Modelling Stand'** 1951

Chalk, pencil and wash on card 37.8 × 24.1 cm (card size)
Given by the artist in the 1980s

14 **Drawing for 'Still Life on Modelling Stand'** 1951

Chalk on paper, 28.8 × 14.9 cm (paper size)
Given by the artist in the 1980s

15 **Carafe** 1951

Inscribed b.r.: 'Clough'
Lithograph 22 × 17.1 cm (image size)
Not editioned; 3 proofs only
Purchased: The artist 1985

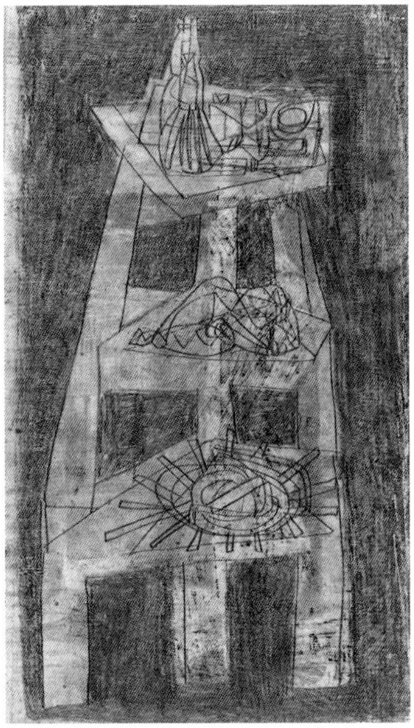

13

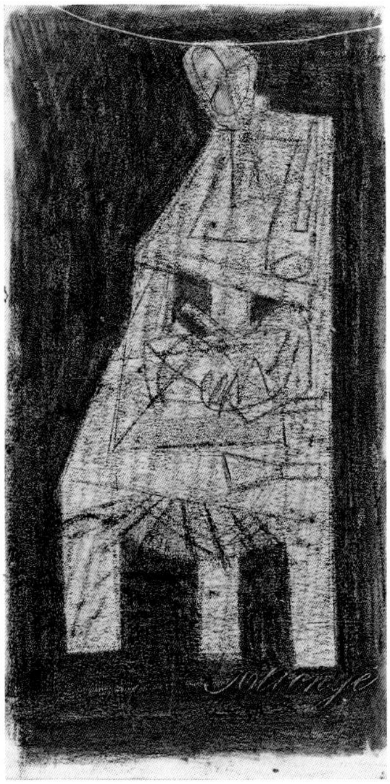

14

16 **Reed on Shore** (or **Sea-Wrack**) 1952

Inscribed b.r: 'Clough'
Lithograph 19.2 × 36.7 cm (image size)
Exhibited: *Contemporary French and English Lithographs*, Redfern Gallery November-December 1952; *British Prints, The Post-War Years, 1945-60*, Redfern Gallery January-February 1986, no.25; *Avant-Garde British Printmaking 1914-1960*, British Museum September 1990-January 1991, no.157
Purchased: The artist

17 **Printer Cleaning Press** 1953 colour plate p.25

Oil on canvas 91.5 × 56.5 cm
Exhibited: *Figures in their Setting*, Contemporary Art Society touring exhibition, 1953, no.10, entitled *Printer Cleaning Forme*. (A postcard from the artist to the collector, dated February 1987, explains that the word 'forme' is only associated with hares, so the title was changed.)
Purchased: Blond Fine Art, London 1986

18 **Sick Woman No.1** 1953

Inscribed b.r.: 'Clough'
Chalk on card 36.8 × 29.2 cm
Exhibited: *Prunella Clough, A Retrospective Exhibition*, Whitechapel Art Gallery, London 1960, no.165; *Moments of Being*, South Bank Centre, London 1988 (touring) [not numbered]
Purchased: JPL Fine Arts, London 1976

19 **Woman in a Factory** c.1953-4

Inscribed b.r.: 'Clough'
Watercolour and charcoal on paper 16.2 × 13.5 cm (image size)
Given by the artist 1990

20 **Untitled** 1950s

Inscribed b.l.: 'Artist's proof' and b.r.: 'Clough'
Etching and aquatint 21.4 × 21.4 cm (image size)
Not editioned
Purchased: The artist 1985

21 **Untitled** 1950s

Inscribed b.l.: 'A/P' and b.r.: 'Clough'
Etching and aquatint 21.7 × 17.5 cm (image size)
Not editioned
Purchased: The artist 1985

22 **Untitled** 1961

Inscribed b.r.: 'Clough'
Monoprint 30.6 × 30.1 cm (image size)
Exhibited: Matthiesen Gallery, London 1962 (One of a group of c.20-22 monoprints, all done in 1961, shown in this exhibition.)
Purchased: Monika Kinley 1975

23 **Untitled** 1961

Inscribed b.r.: 'Clough'
Monoprint 30.7 × 30.3 cm (image size)
Exhibited: Matthiesen Gallery 1962, no.4
Purchased: Monika Kinley 1975

24 **Untitled** 1961

Inscribed b.r.: 'Clough'
Monoprint 30.8 × 30.5 cm (image size)
Exhibited: Matthiesen Gallery 1962, no.20
Purchased: Monika Kinley 1975

25 **Men at Work** 1960s

Portfolio of eighteen drawings and monoprints

a. Inscribed b.r.: 'Clough'
Pencil and watercolour on paper 25.2 × 19.8 cm

b. Inscribed b.r.: 'Clough'
Pencil and watercolour on paper 25.2 × 19.8 cm

c. Inscribed b.r.: 'Clough'
Pencil and watercolour on paper 25.3 × 20.3 cm

d. Inscribed b.r.: 'Clough'
Pencil and watercolour on paper 25.2 × 19.8 cm

e. Inscribed b.r.: 'Clough'
Pencil and watercolour on paper 25.3 × 20.3 cm

f. Inscribed b.r.: 'Clough'
Monoprint 17.5 × 10.7 cm

g. Inscribed b.r.: 'Clough'
Monoprint 17.5 × 10.7 cm

h. Inscribed b.l.: 'Clough'
Monoprint 17.5 × 10.7 cm

i. Inscribed b.r.: 'Clough'
Monoprint 17.5 × 10.7 cm

j. Inscribed b.r.: 'Clough'
Monoprint 17.5 × 10.7 cm

k. Inscribed b.l.: 'Clough'
Monoprint 17.5 × 10.7 cm

l. Monoprint 17.5 × 10.7 cm

m. Inscribed b.r.: 'Clough'
Monoprint 20.2 × 12.5 cm

n. Inscribed b.l.: 'Clough'
Monoprint 15.6 × 12.6 cm

o. Inscribed b.l.: 'Clough'
Monoprint 20.3 × 12.6 cm

p. Inscribed b.r.: 'Clough'
Watercolour and crayon on paper 20.3 × 12.6 cm

q. Inscribed b.l.: 'Clough'
Monoprint and watercolour 24 × 20.1 cm

r. Inscribed b.l.: 'Clough'
Monoprint 12.7 × 11 cm
Given by the artist c.1990

Prunella Clough was born in London in 1919, the niece of Eileen Gray, the designer. She studied at Chelsea School of Art 1938-9 and then, during the War, worked as a mapping and engineering draughtsman. At this time she was friendly with artists like Robert Colquhoun, Robert MacBryde and Keith Vaughan, described as Neo-Romantics, but her early work is distinguished by its gritty realism. From 1946-50 she drew her subjects from working ports in East Anglia, (see no.10, *Man Filleting Fish*), and in 1951 exhibited a large picture of *Lowestoft Harbour*, showing fish merchants weighing fish, in the Arts Council's exhibition of commissioned works for the Festival of Britain. Then followed more scenes of workers such as printers (see no.17) and lorry drivers and of industrial landscapes seen in the Midlands and in London where she has always worked. In 1960 she had a retrospective exhibition at the Whitechapel Art Gallery. The introduction to the catalogue of this exhibition by Michael Middleton remains the most informative discussion of her realist period.

Afterwards her work gradually became more abstract and an interest in Dubuffet and Ernst perhaps led her to exploit paint as a suggestive rather than merely descriptive medium. Her colour has also lightened and become more luminous. Whereas her early work was firmly earthbound, locked into the grey industrial world, her most recent work recalls the rainbow hued 'thought forms' of the theosophists who inspired Kandinsky.

Catalogue introduction by M. Middleton to *Prunella Clough, A Retrospective Exhibition*, Whitechapel Art Gallery, London 1960
M. Yorke, *The Spirit of Place*, London 1988
F. Carey and A. Griffiths, *Avant-Garde British Printmaking, 1914-1960*, British Museum 1990
Prunella Clough, *Recent Painting 1980-1989*, Annely Juda Fine Art, London 1989

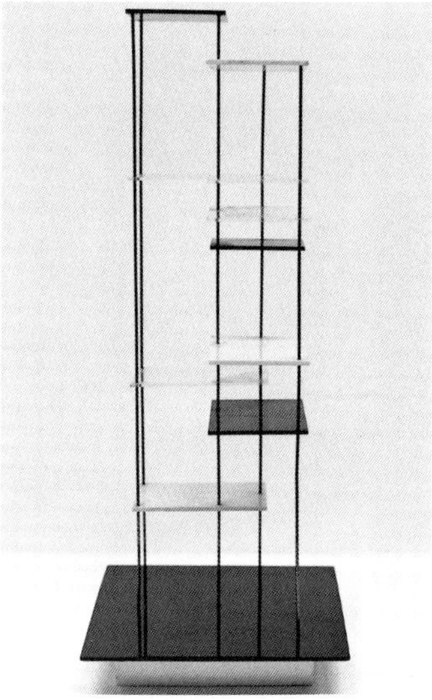

26

JOHN ERNEST b.1922

26 Maquette for a Tower 1955

Inscribed beneath base: 'ERNEST 1955'
Plastic, steel wire and perspex 33 cm high
Exhibited: The tower, for which this is a maquette, was exhibited at *This is Tomorrow*, Whitechapel Art Gallery, London 1956. The maquette, which appears to have been slightly altered since, is illustrated in the catalogue. *British Sculpture in the 20th Century, Part 2 : Symbol and Imagination 1951-1980*, Whitechapel Art Gallery November 1981-January 1982, no.58
Given by the artist 1974

27 Strip Relief IV 1962

Formica, stainless steel, cellulose, wood 75.7 × 109 cm
Exhibited: *Kompas II : Contemporary Paintings in London*, Stedelijk Van Abbemuseum, Eindhoven 1962; *Corsham Painters and Sculptors*, Arts Council touring exhibition 1965, no.51; *John Ernest, Constructions 1955-64*, Institute of Contemporary Arts, London July-August 1964, no.13; *John Ernest*, Arnolfini Gallery, Bristol October 1966, no.6
Purchased: The artist through the Arnolfini Gallery, Bristol 1974

John Ernest was born in Philadelphia in 1922. He studied and worked in New York and served in the merchant marine before moving to Europe, first to Sweden and then France. In 1951 he came to London from Paris and between 1952 and 1956 studied sculpture at St. Martin's School of Art. Here he met Robert Adams and Kenneth Martin and renewed acquaintance with Victor Pasmore whom he had met earlier in Paris. Ernest's sculptures of that period are carved from solid wood, while his paintings have dense, opaque surfaces and basic geometric shapes similar to those in Gilbert's and Constant's work of 1952-3.

In 1954 Ernest started to show with Pasmore's circle, beginning with the exhibition *Artist v. Machine* where he exhibited a constructed tower of plywood and dowel. This was the first of several tower constructions. Two more were shown at *This is Tomorrow* in 1956. These were of plastic sheet and metal rod. (No.26 is a maquette for one of them.) Ernest's largest tower, made of builder's steel scaffolding, was erected as a landmark for the

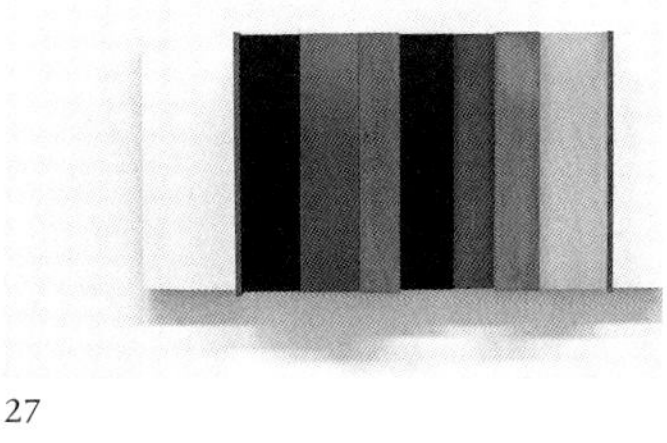

27

Sixth Congress of the International Union of Architects on the South Bank, London in 1961.

Like Anthony Hill, with whom he collaborated in *This is Tomorrow*, Ernest also started to make relief constructions in the mid-fifties. Over the next decade he developed several types of relief using industrial sheet materials, a 'Strip' series (see no.27), an 'L' series and a 'Mosaic' series. They depend for their effect on the juxtaposition of carefully selected and finished modern materials in balanced, asymmetric formations. Ernest showed them in the exhibitions devoted to constructed abstract art in Britain and abroad which are listed in the chronology.

Much of Ernest's time was also taken up with designing and making scientific models and with teaching, at Corsham from 1960-64 and from 1960 also at Chelsea. Through his teaching he influenced younger constructionists such as Terry Pope and John Law. His rate of production, never fast because of his painstaking craftsmanship, slowed by the late sixties. His rare later works translate mathematical concepts, such as group theory, into art.

This is Tomorrow, Whitechapel Art Gallery, London 1956
J. Ernest, 'A Review of Synthesis' [in fact a statement], *Gazette* no.1, 1961, p.3
John Ernest, Constructions 1955-64, Institute of Contemporary Arts, London 1964
John Ernest, Arnolfini Gallery, Bristol 1966
J. Ernest, 'Symmetry', *Structure* III, no.1, 1960, pp.9-16
J. Ernest, 'Some Thoughts on Mathematics', *Structure* III, no.2, 1961, pp.48-53
Constructive Context, Arts Council touring exhibition 1978

TERRY FROST b.1915

28 **Pink Quay** 1956 colour plate p.26

Oil on board 91.5 × 104 cm
Exhibited: *Terry Frost, Retrospective Exhibition*, Laing Art Gallery, Newcastle-upon-Tyne 1964, no.19; New Art Centre, London 1985
Purchased: New Art Centre, London 1985

Frost was encouraged to paint by Adrian Heath while a prisoner of war in Stalag 383. In 1946 he settled in Cornwall but from 1947-50, at Heath's suggestion, studied at Camberwell School of Art. Here, the teaching of Victor Pasmore and Kenneth Martin led him, by 1949, to start abstract paintings and collages using harmonious divisions of the rectangle. His friendship with members of Pasmore's circle in London, particularly Heath, was maintained during the next decade and Frost showed in many of their early abstract art exhibitions, though in 1950 he had returned to live in St. Ives, working for a time for Barbara Hepworth. In *Nine Abstract Artists*, to which Frost was the only contributor from Cornwall, Alloway remarked: 'In St. Ives they combine non-figurative theory with the practice of abstraction because the landscape is so nice nobody can quite bring themselves to leave it out of their art .' (*Nine Abstract Artists*, p.12). This is true of an important early painting by Frost, *Walk along the Quay* of 1950, in which the format of the canvas and the linked semi-circles and stepped rectangles of its composition evoke rocking boats and the quay itself. Frost's reliance on his senses, stimulated by particular moments of observation, led Heath, as recently as 1986, to label his friend a Romantic. (*Terry Frost, Painting in the 1980s*, University of Reading 1985, p.13)

From 1952-4 Frost taught at Corsham with Lanyon, Armitage and Scott and from 1954-6 he worked in Leeds as a Gregory Fellow. Frost's *Pink Quay* (no.28) may reflect the stone-walled fields and also, perhaps, the rows of red-brick back-to-backs of his Yorkshire environment, but the title seems to suggest references to Cornwall. In 1957 Frost came close to Hilton, they visited Paris together in that year, and their paintings of the late fifties have similar freely brushed forms and colours evocative of figures and landscape. In 1960, when he had a one-man exhibition at the Bertha Schaefer Gallery in New York, Frost met American artists supported by Greenberg. His paintings of the sixties are in some ways a hand-crafted critique of Noland's sophisticated circles and chevrons.

L. Alloway, *Nine Abstract Artists,* London 1954
Terry Frost, Paintings, Drawings and Collages, Arts Council of Great Britain and South West Arts 1976-77
Terry Frost, Painting in the 1980s, University of Reading 1986

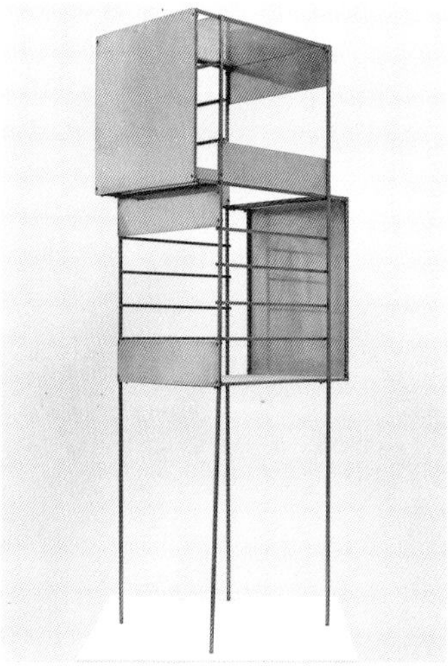

30

STEPHEN GILBERT b.1910

29 **Untitled** 1953

Inscribed b.l.: 'Epreuve d'artiste' and b.r.: 'Stephen Gilbert'
Lithograph 32 × 39.5 cm (paper size)
One of a suite of *Douze lithographes originales en couleurs*, printed by Jean Pons of Paris, published in 1953, with an introduction by R. V. Gindertael, in an edition of 100 and 13 artist's proofs lettered 'A' to 'N'. This proof is 'A'. Gilbert organised the publication to which Hilton and Constant also contributed.
Purchased: William Weston Gallery, London 1976

30 **Construction with Aluminium Plates** 1954

Aluminium and steel, 95 cm high
Exhibited: *The Non-Objective World, 1939-1955*, Annely Juda Fine Art, London July-September 1972, no.69
Purchased: Annely Juda Fine Art, London 1975

Stephen Gilbert was born in 1910 of English parents, the grandson of the sculptor Sir Alfred Gilbert. From 1929-32 he attended the Slade School in London where he met Roger Hilton and Jocelyn Chewett, his future wife. In 1939 Gilbert established himself in Paris but in 1940, having been turned down for military service, he went to Ireland where he stayed for the duration of the War. There he painted Surrealist/Expressionist works, inspired by reading Jung, Nietzsche and Jakob Böhme, which he showed in 1945 at the White Stag Gallery in Dublin. He returned to Paris in 1946 where he continued a series of paintings of spectral, symmetrical insects.

Some of these paintings at the *Salon des Surindépendents* in 1948 attracted the attention of the Danish artist Asger Jorn who enrolled Gilbert as a member of the international group COBRA.

Of the group, Gilbert was closest to Constant and together in the early fifties they developed abstract paintings of loose geometric forms, restricting their palettes in 1951 almost entirely to black and white. Together in Holland they studied Mondrian, Malevich and Rietveld and, in the face of the rising tide of *tachisme* in Paris, structured their pictures of 1952-3 with geometric planes coloured with primary colours on white. Gilbert's lithograph (no.29) is based on a painting of 1952 which owes a clear debt to Malevich.

In 1953-4 Gilbert moved from painting to three-dimensional, orthogonal constructions. He joined the *Groupe Espace* and with Constant, Nicholas Schöffer and the architect Claude Parent formed a subsidiary group called *Néovision*. Strongly influenced by *De Stijl* ideas, they aimed to destroy closed volumes and activate open space by means of coloured planes. Though uncoloured, the aluminium construction of 1954 in Powell's collection (no.30), with its play of positive / negative planes arranged to encourage the spectator to move from one façade to the next, is a good example of their work at this time. In 1955 Gilbert moved further towards an architectural realization of his spatial theory with a model for a House Néovision to be built in Yorkshire by Peter Stead, a developer to whom Gilbert had been introduced by Hilton. Further projects followed in 1956 for blocks of flats to be made of coloured metal panels and insulated glass but in the end only one house was built by Stead, without Gilbert's collaboration. Gilbert himself continued to develop his constructions, introducing planes with curved edges in 1955 and in 1957 abandoning rectilinear frames and letting coloured planes, in reacting curves, stand on their own.

S. Gilbert, 'Notes on Orthogonal and Curvilinear Space-Form', *Structure* 5th series, part 2, 1963, pp.33-35
A. Hill (ed.), *DATA. Directions in Art, Theory and Aesthetics*, London 1968
Stephen Gilbert, Structures 1962-65, Hamilton Galleries, London 1965
Stephen Gilbert, Sculpture of the 60s and Works on Paper, The Belgrave Gallery, London 1992

ADRIAN HEATH 1920-1992

31 **Climbing Composition Green and Blue** 1950

colour plate p.27

Inscribed on reverse: 'CLIMBING / Composition Green and Blue / ; 1950 / AH / 32" × 20"'
Oil on canvas 81.5 × 50.6 cm
Exhibited: *Abstract Painting, Sculptures, Mobiles;* A.I.A. Gallery, London May-June 1951, no.15 (titled *Blue Abstract*)
Reproduced: L. Alloway, *Nine Abstract Artists*, London 1954 pl.14 (not 13 as captioned), with the title *Climbing Composition in Blue*
Purchased: The artist 1974

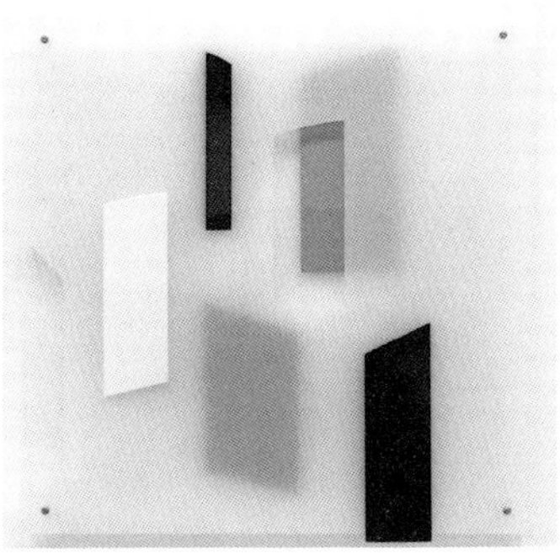

32

32 **Light Screen** 1954-82

Perspex and plastic 55.5 × 55.5 cm
Exhibition of original: ; *Artist v. Machine*, Building Centre, London May-June 1954; *The Non-Objective World 1939-1955*, Annely Juda Fine Art, London July-September 1972, no.76
This is a facsimile of the original which was damaged in two places and presented to the Tate Gallery Archive in 1983. (See *Tate Gallery Illustrated Biennial Report 1982-84*, p.76.) The second version was made by Stanley Bishop in 1982.

Heath's training at the Slade School, London was broken by the War in which he served in the RAF and was taken prisoner. After the War he completed his academic training at the Slade and then spent a year painting realist landscapes and portraits at Carcassonne in southern France. There he was struck by Jacques Villon's work seen in reproduction, which led him in 1948, on his return to England, 'to synthesize the visual image within a harmonic divison of the canvas'. (Undated typescript from the artist.) He renewed friendship with Terry Frost and Victor Pasmore and in 1949 met Kenneth and Mary Martin and Anthony Hill. At Pasmore's request he showed his first abstract composition at the London Group in December of that year but did not fully commit himself to abstract art until 1951 when he became one of the most active members of Pasmore's circle.

In May 1961 Heath helped to organize the first postwar exhibition in Britain devoted to abstract art, at the A.I.A., where he showed the painting in Powell's collection (no.31). It hung with paintings by Kenneth and Mary Martin, Frost, Hill and Pasmore himself, which are related in style. Crucial for them all were the theories of harmonious proportion and dynamic composition of Hambidge, Power and Ghyka (listed in the bibliography at the end of the catalogue). Heath, particularly impressed by Hambidge, based his compositions on divisions of root rectangles. With trial pieces of cut card, which he rotated and shifted, he created a sense of constructed movement, of organic growth.

In 1952-3 Heath organized further group exhibitions in his own studio at 22 Fitzroy Street, and in 1953 published a succinct history of abstract art (*Abstract Painting, its Origins and Meaning*, London). He was also largely responsible for the publication and accompanying exhibition *Nine Abstract Artists* in 1954-5. By this date several of his friends had moved from painting into three-dimensional constructions of industrial materials. In c.1954, Heath himself experimented with reliefs in plastic of which the *Light Screen* (no.32) seems to be the only one surviving. It was shown in its first version in an exhibition held at the Building Centre in 1954 which aimed to demonstrate how artists could use industrial materials creatively. The *Light Screen* does not resemble the reliefs of Pasmore or Mary Martin, examples of which where shown in the same exhibition, but recalls those made by Moholy-Nagy in the thirties. Its planes, which seems to advance from the background through the foreground surface into the spectator's own space, also resemble those in Kupka's paintings of c.1912 which Heath admired. There is a forerunner in his own work in an uncharacteristic oil of 1951-2, inspired by the pattern of waves advancing to the beach in St. Ives. (See *St. Ives 1939-64*, Tate Gallery 1985, no.107).

Following the exhibition *Nine Abstract Artists* in 1955, Heath continued to show with Pasmore's circle but in c.1956-7 he started to use more textured surfaces and freer forms within oval formats. In 1957-8, perhaps through life-classes at Corsham, where he had started to teach, references to the nude and to landscape can be detected in his work. After the *Dimensions* exhibition in December 1957 he ceased to show with the constructivists. He remained a prolific painter, as well as an admired and much sought-after teacher and adviser, until his recent death.

L. Alloway, *Nine Abstract Artists*, London 1954
Adrian Heath, Retrospective Exhibition, City Art Gallery, Bristol 1971
Adrian Heath, Works on Paper. Austin/Desmond Fine Art, London n.d.[1990]

PATRICK HERON b.1920

33 Green Night 1958

Lithograph 64.5 × 50.8 cm (paper size)
Proof copy printed by Stanley Jones in St. Ives apart from the edition of (probably) 30
Purchased: New Art Centre, London 1986

34 Blue Painting (Squares and Disc) 1958-9

colour plate p.28

Inscribed on the stretcher: 'Patrick Heron Blue Painting (Squares and Disc)/ August '58-February '59'
Oil on canvas 152.4 × 121.5 cm
Exhibited: *Four English Middle Generation Painters*, Waddington Galleries, London 1965, no.24 (illustrated); *English Contrasts*, Artcurial, Paris September-November 1984
Purchased: New Art Centre, London 1985

In 1958, the year he started the painting and made the print in Powell's collection, Heron wrote: 'My main interest, in my painting, has always been in colour, space and light ... and space in colour is the *subject* of my painting today to the exclusion of everything else. But the space must never be too *deep*, or the colour too flat. Each painting has to adjust depth to surface in a new and unique manner.' (Quoted in *Patrick Heron, Recent Paintings and Selected Earlier Canvases*, Whitechapel Art Gallery, London 1972, n.p.n.)

Since he started as an artist before the War, designing for his father's Cresta Silks, he has exploited the liberated colour of modern French painters, such as Bonnard, Braque and especially the *Fauves*. In 1943-4 he was able to look long and hard at Matisse's

Red Studio which was then at the Redfern Gallery in London. After the War he wrote eloquently about the qualities he admired in French art and in avant-garde British artists such as Hitchens, Lanyon and Hilton.

Apart from a few experimental paintings in de Staël's manner in 1952, Heron did not develop abstract compositions until 1956. He exhibited these abstract 'garden' paintings and his first 'stripe' paintings at the *Metavisual Tachiste Abstract* exhibition at the Redfern Gallery in April 1957. Coupled with unfettered colour he used brushmarks to modulate space. As he wrote later : 'The mere brushwork of an area endows it with differing kinds of space-creating power.' (Whitechapel, 1972, n.p.n.) Though he wrote appreciatively of the new American painting when it appeared in London in 1956 he was not totally converted. Two years later he remarked that he missed, even in Rothko, the Abstract Expressionist he most admired, 'a sensuous subtlety of tone colour, a subtle asymmetry of shape, a varied tempo of working.' (*Patrick Heron*, Barbican Art Gallery, 1985, p.10).

In canvases of 1957-8, and the lithograph shown here (no.33), freely brushed rectangles of colour shift in relation to each other, their edges parallel to those of the rectangular fields. A little later, in pictures of 1958-9 such as no.34, done soon after Heron had moved into Ben Nicholson's old studio, one or two rectangles have had their corners squashed. The almost circular forms hold their positions on the canvas with more tension than the rectangular ones whose space they share.

Heron had his first one-man exhibition at Downing's Bookshop, St. Ives and at the Redfern Gallery in 1947. He continued to exhibit at the Redfern until 1959 when he moved to the Waddington Galleries where he had his most recent one-man exhibition in the summer of 1992. He has held retrospective exhibitions in 1967 at the Richard Demarco Gallery, Edinburgh, in 1972 at the Whitechapel Art Gallery and in 1985 at the Barbican Art Gallery.

Patrick Heron, Recent Paintings, Whitechapel Art Gallery, London 1972
St. Ives 1939-64, Tate Gallery 1985
Patrick Heron, Barbican Art Gallery, London 1985

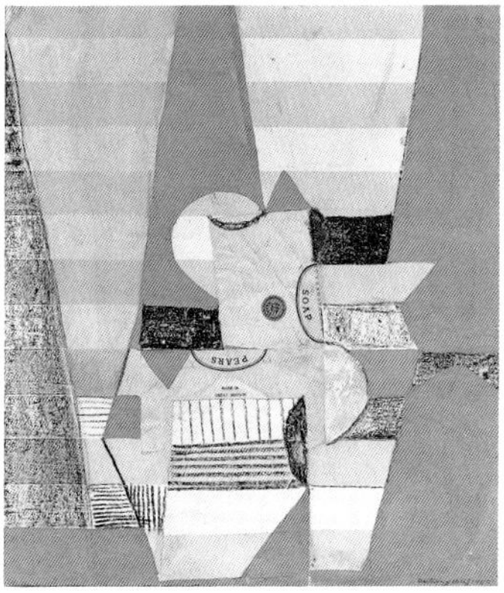

35

ANTHONY HILL b.1930

35 **Composition** 1950

Inscribed b.r.: 'Anthony Hill / 1950'
Collage, crayon, gouache on paper 50.6 × 44.9 cm
Exhibited: Artists' Market Association, Warehouse Gallery, Covent Garden, London 9 February 1978; *Anthony Hill, A Retrospective Exhibition*, Hayward Gallery, London May-July 1983, no.5
Purchased: The artist 1975

36 **Untitled** 1950 illustrated on back cover

Oil on canvas with collage 52.7 × 36.4 cm
Purchased: The artist 1991

37 **Jeux** 1951-83

Inscribed b.r.: 'Anthony Hill 1951-83'
Screenprint 66.5 × 66.5 cm (paper size)
Artist's proof from an edition of 125 and 25 artist's proofs, published by Fausta Squatriti, Milan 1983
Purchased: Contemporary Art Society, London 1983

38 **Orthogonal Composition** 1954

Inscribed on reverse: 'ORTHOGONAL / COMPOSITION / 1953-54 / ANTHONY HILL'
Oil on canvas 137 × 61 cm
Exhibited: Hayward Gallery 1983, no.21
Purchased: The artist 1978
Reproduced: L. Alloway, *Nine Abstract Artists*, London 1954, no.25

39 **Relief Construction** 1956-61

Inscribed on reverse: 'AH / 1960 Anthony Hill 56-61'
Aluminium, plastic, wood and perspex 45.6 × 72.3 cm
Exhibited: *Anthony Hill / Gillian Wise*, Institute of Contemporary Arts, London February 1963, no.2; Hayward Gallery 1983, no.34
Purchased: The artist 1970s

40 **Relief Construction** 1957-70

Inscribed on reverse: 'AH / 57-70'
Copper, aluminium, plastic and perspex 38.2 × 38.2 cm
Exhibited: Hayward Gallery 1983, no.44 (dated 1957-76)
Purchased: The artist 1970s

38

See also no.72 executed jointly with Gillian Wise.

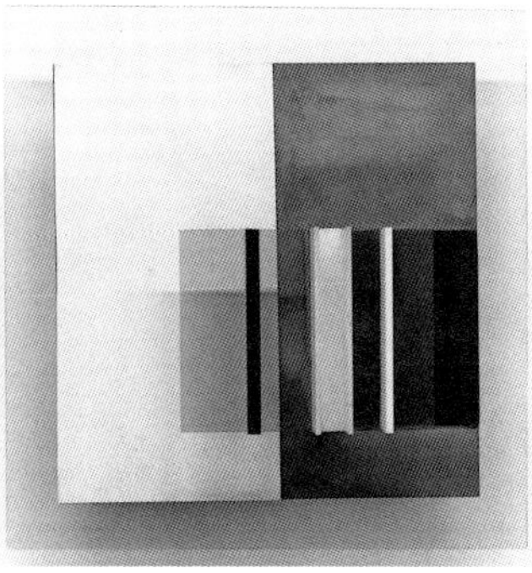
40

Hill met Victor Pasmore and Robert Adams at the Central School, London in 1949. Though he was by far the youngest member of Pasmore's circle, he soon became one of the most active organizers of their exhibitions of new abstract art. He also made important contacts with artists abroad, visiting Paris regularly where he met, among others, Vantongerloo, Kupka, and Stephen Gilbert, and corresponding with Max Bill and Charles Biederman.

The two works of 1950 in Powell's collection (nos.35 and 36), made when Hill was twenty, betray the Cubist influence of Gris as well as of Pasmore's first abstract compositions with connected segments of circles, triangles and rectangles. Hill has wittily found these forms in the wrappers of Pears soap bars. Dadaist appropriation of found materials remained important to him and significantly in 1951 he started to correspond with Marcel Duchamp. He admired particularly Duchamp's formal innovations, his use of industrial materials, his renunciation of oil paint. Hill also strove for an impersonal finish and painted *Jeux*, on which the print in Powell's collection is based (no. 37) in a shiny enamel paint (Ripolin). When exhibited in 1952 it was entitled *Prototype for Commercial Reproduction*.

From 1953-6 Hill worked entirely in black and white. He

constructed positive / negative areas with rhythmic curves and right angles, rigorously opposing the irrational gesture. Powell's fine *Orthogonal Composition* (no.38) was painted in the summer of 1954 and reproduced later that year in *Nine Abstract Artists*. It is the first of a series of tall, narrow, black and white paintings which continue to the New Year of 1956. At the same time Hill experimented with a variety of industrial materials in constructed reliefs. He searched out samples of sheet plastics and in the spring of 1956 started to use L-shaped aluminium angles. He stopped painting and used these 'found' materials for the rest of the decade. He selected them for their varying tonal and light-reflecting qualities and he combined them in orthogonal groupings with an asymmetric balance. In 1960 he wrote in the journal *Structure*:

> *A constructional relief neither stands like sculpture nor is it suspended like mobiles and other kinds of constructions, it is not a window or carpet like a painting and neither is it part of the wall.*
> *The relief is the real plastic object par excellence, it has the dimensions of everyday objects and yet it is not to be confused with them.*
> (Quoted, Hayward Gallery, 1983, p.26)

From c.1960 Hill sought for a more mathematical basis for his art. He continued to use industrial materials, concentrating in the seventies on shallow reliefs of engraved plastic laminate. In 1973 he also began making collages under the name REDO, a Dadaist alter ego.

L. Alloway, *Nine Abstract Artists*, London 1954
A. Hill (ed), *DATA, Directions in Art, Theory and Aesthetics*, London 1968
Anthony Hill, A Retrospective Exhibition, Hayward Gallery, London 1983

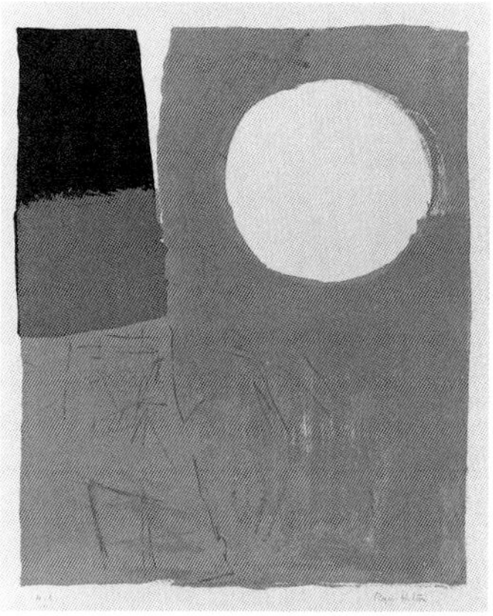

41

ROGER HILTON 1911-1975

41 **Untitled** 1953

Inscribed b.l.: 'H.C.' and b.r.: 'Roger Hilton'
Lithograph 40 × 32.5 cm (paper size)
Purchased: William Weston Gallery, London 1976

42 **Painting February-March 1954** 1954
illustrated on front cover

Oil on canvas 152.5 × 127 cm
Exhibited: *Nine Abstract Artists*, Redfern Gallery, London January 1955, no.15; Special display of Roger Hilton, Tate Gallery August-October 1992
Purchased: Waddington Galleries, London 1987
Reproduced: L. Alloway *Nine Abstract Artists*, London 1954, no.31

Hilton studied at the Slade School, London (1929-31) where he met Stephen Gilbert who remained a friend. In the thirties he spent time in Paris where he was taught by Roger Bissière. He returned there frequently after the War, in which he served in the army, and his first abstract paintings of c.1950 resemble the painterly, linear, mosaic compositions of the French *tachiste* Manessier. Although these paintings were different from those of Pasmore and his circle,

Hilton was included in their early exhibitions of abstract art in London in 1951 at the A.I.A. and at Gimpel Fils, where he had his first one-man exhibition the following year. Gilbert had introduced him to the Dutch former COBRA artist Constant Nieuwenhuys and in February 1953 Hilton visited Holland with Constant (as he was always known) and was impressed by the positive colours on white grounds in Mondrian's paintings. No doubt the space-generating forms in Malevich's Suprematist paintings, which Constant would have shown him on the same trip, also impressed him. They went on to Paris where both made lithographs for a set which Gilbert was organizing, (see no.41). It seems likely that Poliakoff, who also contributed to this set, was another important influence on Hilton at this time. Hilton's lithograph has larger, flatter and more geometric forms than those in his earlier paintings.

The paintings of 1953-4 which he illustrated in *Nine Abstract Artists* – no.42 is one of them – develop this assertive style. In his accompanying statement he wrote:

> *I have a taste for plain pictures; I like my colours dynamic and strongly contrasted.*
> (*Nine Abstract Artists*, 1954, p.30)

L. Alloway, *Nine Abstract Artists*, London 1954
P. Heron, *The Changing Forms of Art*, London 1955
Roger Hilton, the Early Years 1911-1955, Leicester Polytechnic Gallery 1984
St. Ives 1939-64, Tate Gallery 1985

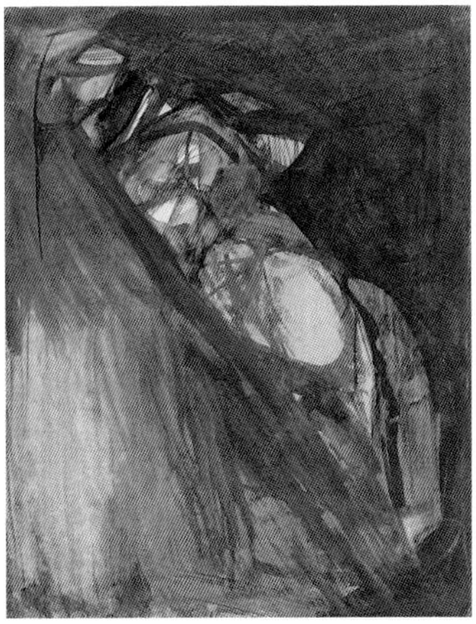
43

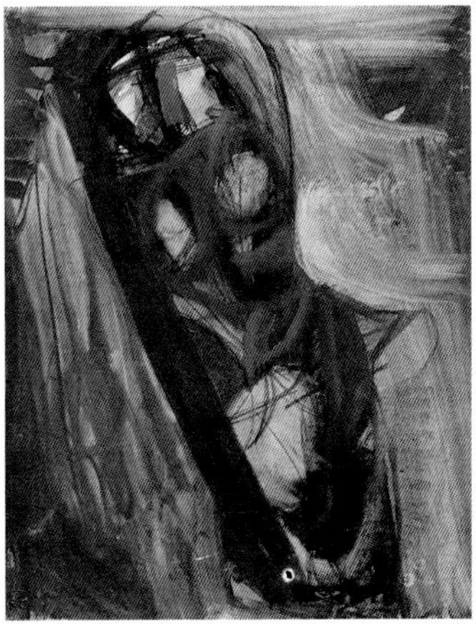
44

PETER LANYON 1918-1964

43 **Red Body Country No.1** 1952

Gouache on paper 58.2 × 46.9 cm
Purchased: Phillips, London 30 November 1987, lot 323

44 **Red Body Country No.2** 1952

Gouache on paper 57.5 × 46.2 cm
Purchased: Redfern Gallery, London 1985

45 **Bantam on Guard** 1953

Mixed media on paper 75 × 44.7 cm
Exhibited: Gimpel Fils, London 1954
Purchased: New Art Centre, London 1982

46 **Nude** 1956

Charcoal on paper 49 × 70.6 cm
Exhibited: *Corsham, A Celebration, the Bath Academy of Art 1946-72*, Victoria Art Gallery, Bath 1988-9, no.71
Purchased: New Art Centre, London 1987

47 **Untitled** 1958

Inscribed b.l.: 'Peter Lanyon 14 March 1958'
Lithograph 46 × 31.2 cm (image size)
Not editioned
Purchased: New Art Centre, London 1980

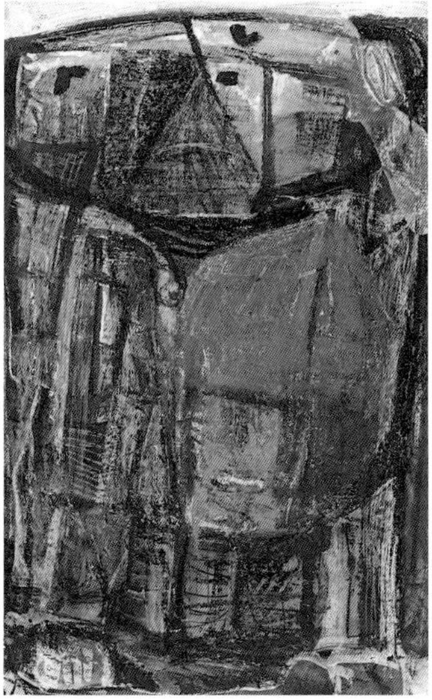
45

48 **Longshore** 1962 colour plate p.29

Inscribed on reverse: 'LONG SHORE / Lanyon 62'
Oil on canvas 183 × 121.7 cm
Exhibited: Premio Marzotto touring exhibition 1962-3, no.54; 4th John Moores Exhibition, Liverpool 1963, no.50; *Profile 3*, Bochum 1964, no.93; Gimpel and Hanover Galerie, Zurich 1964, no.8; St. Ives touring exhibition in Japan 1989, no.55
Purchased: Austin Desmond Fine Art, London 1988

It is remarkable that Lanyon, who trained in 1938 at the painstakingly realist Euston Road School and was then in close contact with the precise, linear, constructivist artists Gabo and Nicholson, should develop after the War into Britain's most forceful gestural painter. In the same way, it is noteworthy that his deep roots in the landscape and people of Penwith seem to have helped rather than hindered his affinity with the American Abstract Expressionists.

As in Pollock's work of the early and mid-forties, there are mythic references in much of Lanyon's art. Powell's *Bantam on Guard* (no.45) was painted in a village in Italy in 1953 when Lanyon began his very large painting *Europa*, and it seems to share its myth. Lanyon explained that for him the Europa myth was appropriate for the very close animal-human relationship he found in the Italian village and that the large patch of red in the picture, also found in no.45, 'comes from the primitive habit of hanging out a red blanket after nuptials.' (Causey, p.19)

Lanyon also liked the Europa myth because Europa is carried off from the land into the sea by a bull. In Cornwall the artist saw the sea as a male element penetrating the coast through the shafts of abandoned tin mines. Even in late paintings like *Longshore* (no.48) interpenetrating male / female forms occur. This painting also conveys the fusion of the elements. To experience this more intensely himself he took up gliding in 1959, the year in which he also started to paint more on canvas than on the board he had favoured before. In 1963 he said of gliding:

> *The whole purpose of gliding was to get a more complete knowledge of the landscape, and the pictures now combine the elements of land, sea and sky – earth, air and water.*
> (*Peter Lanyon, Drawings and Graphic Work*, City Museum and Art Gallery, Stoke-on-Trent 1981, p.76.)

Lanyon had his first one-man exhibition at Downing's Bookshop, St. Ives in 1947. He had regular one-man exhibitions at Gimpel Fils Gallery from 1952 and at the Catherine Viviano Gallery in New York from 1957. A retrospective exhibition toured England in 1968.

Peter Lanyon, Tate Gallery 1968
A. Causey, *Peter Lanyon: His Painting*, Henley-on-Thames 1971
A. Lanyon, *Peter Lanyon*, 1990 (ed. of 50)

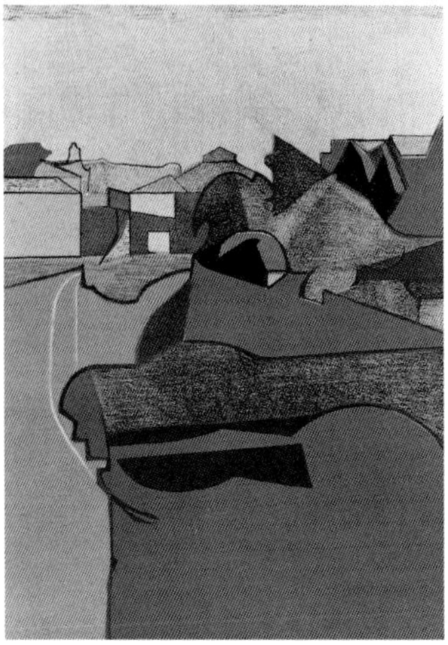

49

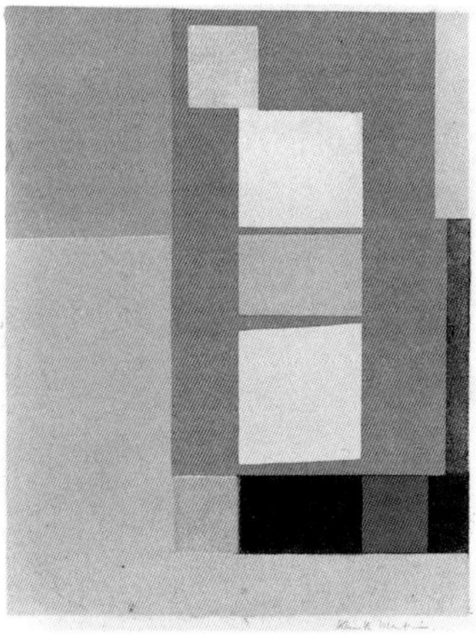

51

52

KENNETH MARTIN 1905-1984

49 **Chalk Farm** 1949

Lithograph 35.3 × 25 cm (image size)
Not editioned, but several proofs made in different colour combinations
Exhibited: *Les Peintres-Graveurs*, Redfern Gallery, London December 1949, no.164; *British Prints, The Post-War Years, 1945-60*, Redfern Gallery January-February 1986, no.70
Purchased: Redfern Gallery, London 1989

50 **Composition** 1949-50 colour plate p.30

Inscribed b.l.: 'Martin'
Oil on canvas 40.8 × 35.3 cm
Exhibited: Leicester Galleries, London August-September 1950 (titled *Abstract, Green and Brown*)
Purchased: New Art Centre, London 1983

51 **Abstract** 1950

Inscribed b.r.: 'Kenneth Martin'
Lithograph 32.2 × 25.6 (image size)
Exhibited: *Society of London Painter-Printers*, Redfern Gallery December 1950-January 1951, no.29; *I. Bienal*, São Paulo, 1951; *First Exhibition of Abstract Art*, 22 Fitzroy Street, London, March 1952; *British Prints, The Post-War Years 1945-60*, Redfern Gallery January-February 1986, no.71; *Avant-Garde British Printmaking 1914-1960*, British Museum 1990, no.180 (illus. in colour)
Purchased: Redfern Gallery, London 1989

52 **Abstract Print** 1956-62

Inscribed b.r.: 'Kenneth Martin'
Linoprint 74.7 × 50.9 (paper size)
Exhibited: *Kenneth Martin, A Retrospective Exhibition*, Lords Gallery, London October-November 1962, no.16 (with above title and date); *Kenneth Martin*, Tate Gallery 1975, no.34 (listed as a lithograph and dated 1961)
Purchased: Annely Juda Fine Art, London 1987
This item has been catalogued with the help of Susan Tebby

53 **Variable (Documenta)** 1968

Inscribed on underside of base: '25/50 / Kenneth Martin'
Brass on painted wood base 16.3 cm high
Exhibited: *Kenneth Martin*, Tate Gallery 1975, no.80
Purchased: Galerie Wilbrand, Cologne

Kenneth Martin changed from painting flat, realist paintings to abstract compositions in 1949. Already his earliest abstract paintings and prints are built up from a sequence of constructive movements. In Powell's painting of 1949-50 (no.50) he has used the golden section to divide the format into units which he rocks across and down. There is a sense of structured events taking place through time, of organic development. The print of 1950 (no.51) is closely related to a painting now in the Tate Gallery which Martin said was inspired by the pattern of cells in a dragon-fly's wing reproduced in D'Arcy Thompson's book *On Growth and Form*. In his brass *Screw Mobiles* begun in 1953, he orders the elements on a simple system such as that discovered by Fibonacci (1, 2, 3, 5, 8, 13, etc). Martin may invert the order to obtain variety, as he explains

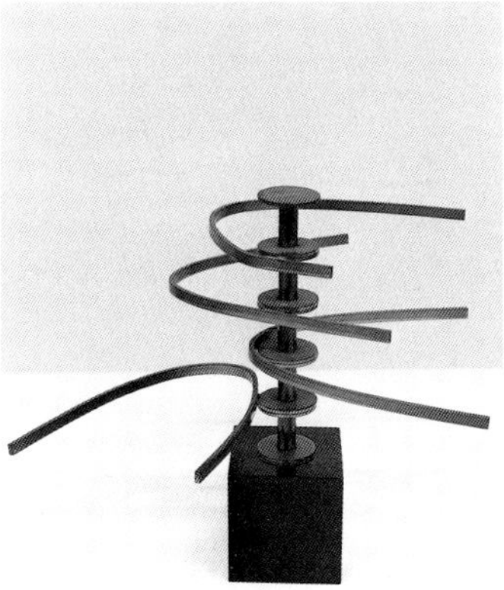

53

in this statement:

An event or a series of events may be ordered by a rhythm. The same event can be repeated varying its temporal or spatial position. An event can be inverted and take on a new, strange character. A whole system can be changed by inversions.

(*Kenneth Martin*, Yale Center for British Art 1979, p.16)

The brass *Variable* (no.53) is a development from two large mobiles Martin made for the *I.U.A. Congress* building on the South Bank in 1961. Parabolic strips are fixed at different points to discs threaded on a vertical spine. It is a multiple, produced at a time when there was an optimistic belief that artworks produced in large numbers would be widely available; yet, because the parabolas can be moved into different positions, each copy is unique.

Kenneth Martin showed in the abstract art exhibitions listed in the chronology. He had an exhibition with Mary Martin at the Heffer Gallery, Cambridge in 1954 and others at the Institute of Contemporary Arts and at Lords Gallery, London in 1960 and 1962 respectively. He started to exhibit at the Waddington Galleries in 1970. There was a major retrospective at the Tate Gallery in 1975.

He has written clearly and extensively about his works.

Kenneth Martin, Tate Gallery 1975
Kenneth Martin, Yale Center for British Art, New Haven 1979
Kenneth and Mary Martin, Annely Juda Fine Art, London 1987

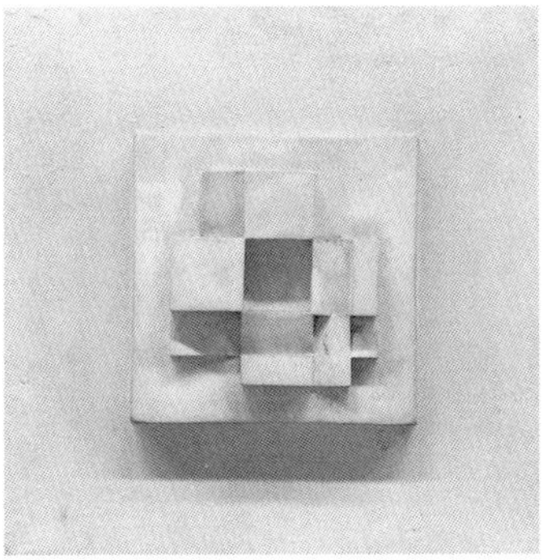

54

MARY MARTIN 1907-1969

54 Spiral Movement 1951-1972

Fibreglass 29.1 × 29.4 cm
Multiple published by the Tate Gallery, London; manufactured by Pan-Art Reproductions, Rugby
Purchased: Tate Gallery, London

55 Rotation 1968

Injected moulded polystyrene and mirrors 12.7 × 12.7 cm
Multiple published by Unlimited, Bath
Purchased: Angela Flowers Gallery, London 1975

Mary Martin, like her husband Kenneth, changed from 'post-impressionist' to abstract painting in 1949-50. Unfortunately her abstract paintings are lost but it seems that her first reliefs, such as *Spiral Movement*, (see no.54), develop from them with their grid compositions based on the square and the golden section. Her son Paul has analysed *Spiral Movement*:

'Spiral Movement' is the combination of a chequerboard motif and a spiralling system of golden section rectangles within it... The system of rectangles starts at the centre then moves in a clockwise direction outwards by 90° turns making a spiral movement ... In 'Spiral Movement' the tilts follow the direction of the spiral and activate the surface.

(*Mary Martin*, Tate Gallery 1984, p.35)

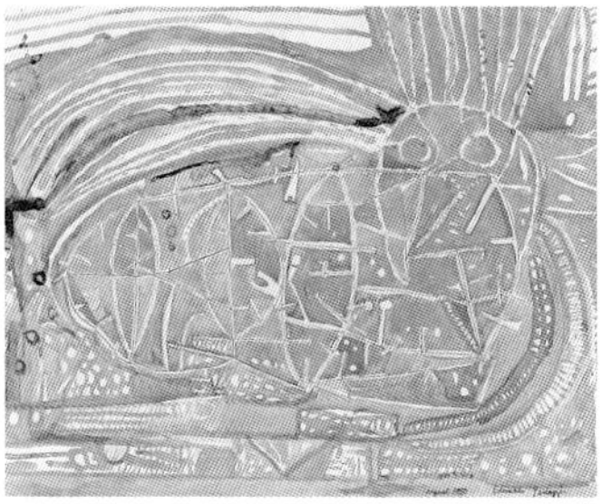

56

Her early reliefs are made of painted wood but from 1954 she employed more industrial materials such as plastic sheet. In 1963 she began to use as a unit in her compositions a half-cube faced with polished stainless steel. She permuted it systematically in rows, building up clusters which reflect together in startling compositions. She realised that her methods and her materials could be adapted easily to architecture and mass production. In 1969 her largest relief, composed of half-cubes faced with polished metal, was erected at the University of Stirling. In the previous year the small *Rotation* multiple went into production by Unlimited. She wrote of multiples:

> *One is making available something which one has reason to believe people would like to possess at the lowest economic price. Multiples are really concerned with the dissemination of ideas, like L.P. records and paperbacks... the ideas of one's own time.*
> (*Mary Martin*, Tate Gallery 1984, p.28)

Mary Martin, Tate Gallery 1984
Kenneth and Mary Martin, Annely Juda Fine Art, London 1987

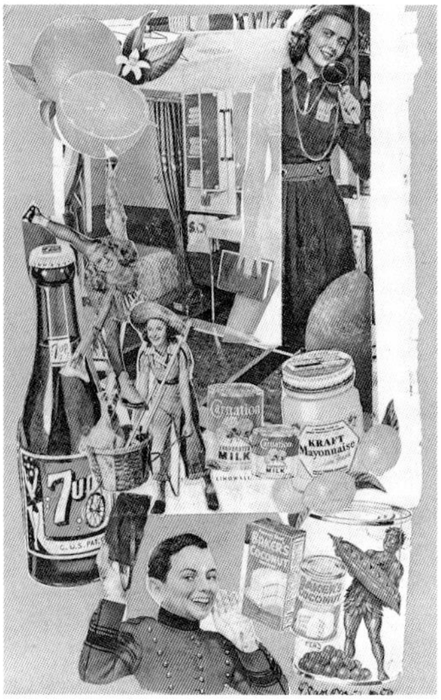

57

EDUARDO PAOLOZZI b.1924

56 Watercolour 1950

Inscribed b.r.: 'August 1950 Eduardo Paolozzi'
Watercolour on paper 55.5 × 69 cm
Exhibited: 17th Biennial, Brooklyn Museum May-June 1953, no.42
Purchased: New Art Centre, London 1976

57 Scrapbook Collage 1950

Inscribed b.r.: 'E Paolozzi 1950'
Collage on paper 38.1 × 24.9 cm
Exhibited: *English Contrasts*, Artcurial, Paris September-November 1984; *The Artful Ad*, Graves Art Gallery, Sheffield 1990
Purchased: The artist 1975

58 Marine Composition 1950

Inscribed b.r. in image: 'July 1950 Eduardo Paolozzi' and b.r. in manuscript: 'Eduardo Paolozzi'
Lithograph 33.7 × 52.7 cm (image size)
Purchased: Sotheby's, London mid-1970s

59 Collage 1951 colour plate p.31

Inscribed b.r.: '1951 Eduardo Paolozzi'
Collage on card 55.2 × 76.1 cm
Exhibited: *Ten Contemporary British Painters*, Sweden 1953, no.37
Purchased: New Art Centre, London 1991; ex. collection of Lilian Somerville

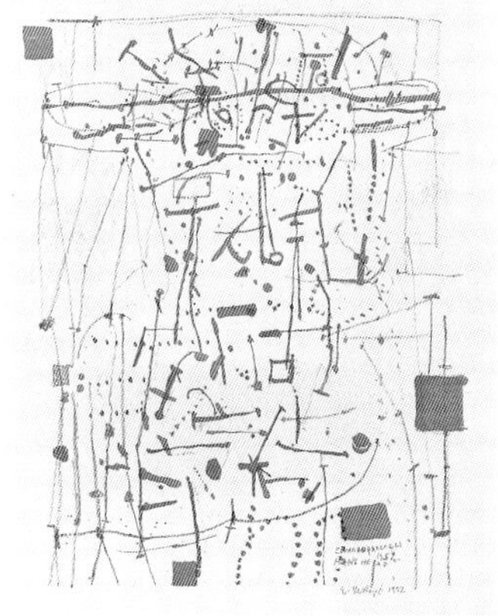

60

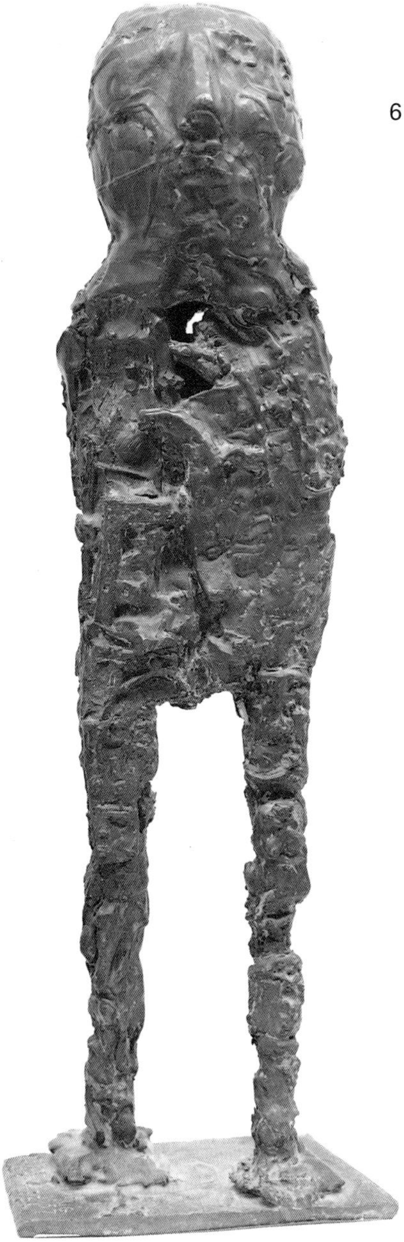

60 **Man's Head** 1952

Inscribed b.r. in image: 'EDUARDO PAOLOZZI / 1952 / MANS HEAD' and b.r. in manuscript: 'E. Paolozzi 1952'
Lithograph 51 × 39 cm (image size)
Exhibited: *Contemporary French and English Lithographs*, Redfern Gallery, London November-December 1952, no. 162; *Avant-Garde British Printmaking 1914-1960*, British Museum 1990, no.225
Purchased: Redfern Gallery, London 1979

61 **Mannikin** 1957

Inscribed in base: 'E. PAOLOZZI AUG 1957'
Bronze 54 cm high
Exhibited: Hanover Gallery, London December 1958, no.14 (dated 1956)
Purchased: Phillips, London, 17 June 1986, no.111

Paolozzi, born in Edinburgh of Italian immigrants, studied at the Slade School in London from 1944-7. Here he disliked the academic teaching but drew from tribal sculpture and Rembrandt in the museums and became friends with fellow students Nigel Henderson and William Turnbull. From 1947-9 Paolozzi was in Paris where he voraciously absorbed the ideas of the late Dadaists and Surrealists and of Dubuffet's *Art Brut*. On his return to Britain he obtained a post teaching textile design at the Central School in London. Powell's lithographs, watercolour and collage (nos.56,58,59 and 60) are similar to his textile designs. Rapidly drawn lines of dots, spokes, plus and minus signs spread across the paper and coalesce into an animal, perhaps a cat, a fish, which has been identified as the living fossil, the coelacanth, and a human head. In contemporary collages, the sense of dislocation, of barely holding together, is further suggested by the way the scraps of paper have been torn and reassembled (no.59). Collages like this were shown at the early abstract art exhibitions organised by Pasmore's circle, though Paolozzi was also strongly drawn to the *Art Brut* espoused by Henderson and the architects Alison and Peter Smithson with whom he organised the remarkable exhibition at the Institute of Contemporary Arts in 1953, *Parallel of Life and Art*. *Parallel of Life and Art* was a collage exhibition of photographs, seemingly juxtaposed at random, of a wide variety of images – details of cells, tribal art, space exploration, the avant-garde paintings of Dubuffet and Pollock.

Paolozzi brought a similar assemblage technique to his sculpture. By pressing found objects into clay and taking a wax cast he was able to bring together fragments of dislocated reality. He assembled these into eroded yet stoic figures such as the *Mannikin* of 1957 (no.61). In 1960 he showed a group of such figures with success at the Venice Biennale.

Eduardo Paolozzi, Arts Council touring exhibition 1976-7
Avant-Garde British Printmaking 1914-1960, British Museum 1990
The Independent Group: Postwar Britain and the Aesthetics of Plenty, Institute of Contemporary Arts, London 1990

VICTOR PASMORE b.1908

62 **Poster for London Group** 1948 colour plate p.32

Lithograph 75.8 × 49.2 cm
Purchased: William Weston Gallery, London

63 **Transparent Relief Construction in White, Black, Green, Lilac and Maroon** 1960-1

Inscribed on reverse: 'VP/Victor Pasmore/1960/61'
Painted wood and perspex 53.3 × 55.8 cm
Exhibited: *Recent Paintings and Constructions by Victor Pasmore*, New London Gallery, London March 1961, no.18 (titled 'Transparent Relief Construction in White, Black, Green and Maroon'); *Victor Pasmore, Retrospective Exhibition 1925-65*, Tate Gallery May-June 1965, no.163
Purchased: Christie's, London 8 November 1985, lot 296; ex. collection of the Hon. Michael Astor

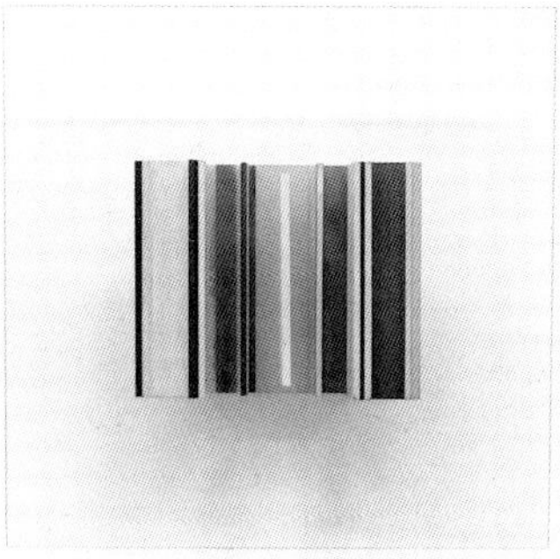
63

Pasmore's poster for the 1948 London Group exhibition (no.62) presented a clear-cut, lively challenge to the prevailing nostalgic Neo-romanticism and stodgy realism of most contemporary British art. Its composition is not abstracted from a natural scene but built up from invented forms arranged on the golden section. In the catalogue to this exhibition he and Elliott Seabrooke, the outgoing president, stated:

> *Today the Group is the only large Society of Painters and Sculptors fully conscious of, and sympathetic with, the developments of Modern Art.*

This was the opening salvo in Pasmore's battle to bring British art abreast of Continental modernism.

Though he and his friends showed together at subsequent London Group exhibitions, their art did not stand out sufficiently from the wide variety of exhibits to make the impact they wanted. So, from 1951, they organized their own exhibitions and accompanying publications devoted to abstract art. Pasmore showed his first constructed reliefs in 1952. The type with vertical slats, such as no.63, was started in 1954, and continued in many different versions to 1961. Though the series owes something to the ideas of Charles Biederman, the grouping of the planes into a rectangular block and the very restricted colour range make them very different from Biederman's reliefs. Pasmore's reliefs are more architectural. In 1956 enlarged versions of the type, of which no.63 is an example, were placed in the Stephenson Engineering Building at the University of Newcastle-upon-Tyne to activate the space in the entrance hall.

Victor Pasmore, Retrospective Exhibition 1925-65, Tate Gallery 1965
Victor Pasmore, Arts Council touring exhibition 1980
A. Bowness and L. Lambertini, *Victor Pasmore, with a Catalogue Raisonné ... 1926-1979*, London 1980

WILLIAM SCOTT 1913-1989

64 **Busby** 1953

Inscribed b.r.: 'William Scott A.P.'
Lithograph 56 × 38.3 cm (paper size)
Artist's proof apart from the edition of 50
Exhibited: *Royal College of Art Coronation Lithographs*, Redfern Gallery, London April-May 1953, no.107; *British Prints, the Post-War Years 1945-60*, Redfern Gallery January-February 1986, no.95; *Corsham, A Celebration, The Bath Academy of Art 1946-72*, Victoria Art Gallery, Bath 1988-9, no.97
Purchased: Redfern Gallery, London 1977

65 **Mingulay** 1962

Inscribed b.r.: 'W. Scott 62 12/75'
Lithograph 49 × 60.9 cm (image size)
Published by Curwen Prints; printed by the Curwen Studio; edition of 75
Purchased: 1976

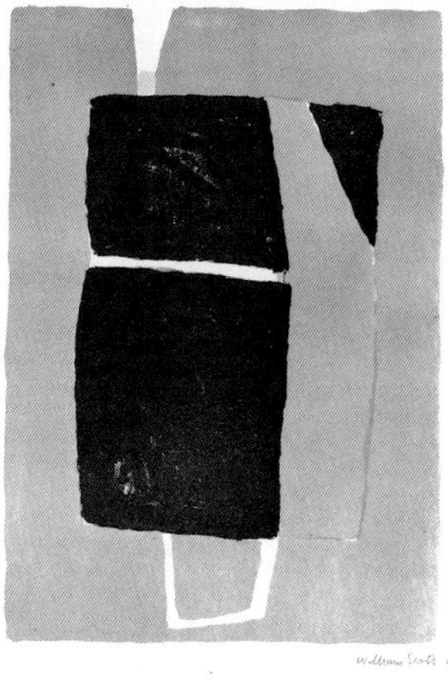

64

Scott was born in Greenock in 1913. His family moved to Northern Ireland in 1924 and Scott trained at Belfast College of Art and then from 1931-5 at the Royal Academy Schools in London. From 1937-9 he lived mainly in France. He served in the army from 1942-6, then became Senior Painting Master at Corsham, a post he held until 1956. He had one-man exhibitions regularly at the Hanover Gallery, London and the Martha Jackson Gallery in New York. He showed at the Venice Biennale in 1958. There were major retrospectives at the Tate in 1972 and at the Ulster Museum, Belfast in 1986 (and subsequent tour).

Scott was producing his most abstract paintings from c.1952-4 when he made the lithograph *Busby* (no.64). Dense, flat, roughly rectangular areas of colour are stretched across the canvas or paper. Bold channels of black or white connect the areas like the handles of the kitchen utensils or the limbs of figures in his less abstract work. *Busby*, as befits a lithograph made to celebrate the Coronation, refers to the guards' bearskin.

Scott visited Cornwall regularly from 1946 and the lithograph *Mingulay* of 1962 can be related to the abstract landscapes of his friends there, particularly Hilton and Lanyon.

A. Bowness, *William Scott, Paintings*, London 1964
William Scott, Paintings, Drawings and Gouaches 1938-71, Tate Gallery 1972
R. Alley and T. P. Flanagan, *William Scott*, The Arts Council of Northern Ireland 1986

JACK SMITH b.1928

66 **Figures and Objects in a Room** 1959

Inscribed b.r.: 'Jack Smith 59' and on reverse: 'FIGURES + OBJECTS IN A ROOM JACK SMITH 59'
Oil on canvas 122.1 × 121.7 cm
Exhibited: *Jack Smith Retrospective*, Whitechapel Art Gallery, London 1959; *British Painting 1952-77*, Royal Academy of Arts, London 1977, no. 328
Purchased: Monika Kinley 1975

67 **Light Movement No. 6** 1962

Inscribed on reverse: 'JACK SMITH 1962 LIGHT MOVEMENT (6)'
Oil on canvas 167.5 × 167.5 cm
Exhibited: Carnegie Institute, Pittsburgh 1963; *Profile 3*, Bochum 1964, no.139; Grosvenor Gallery, London 1965; *Jack Smith, Paintings and Drawings 1949-76*, Sunderland Arts Centre 1977 and touring
Purchased: Monika Kinley 1977

Jack Smith studied at Sheffield College of Art 1944-6 and then at St. Martin's and the Royal College in London 1948-53. He taught at Corsham 1953-6 and then at Chelsea School of Art and other art schools, including Brighton Polytechnic. From 1952-8 he showed regularly at the Beaux Arts Gallery. He had a retrospective exhibition at the Whitechapel Gallery in 1959 and at the Sunderland Arts Centre in 1979 which subsequently toured.

Jack Smith Retrospective, Whitechapel Art Gallery, London 1959
Jack Smith, Paintings and Drawings 1949-76, Sunderland Arts Centre 1977

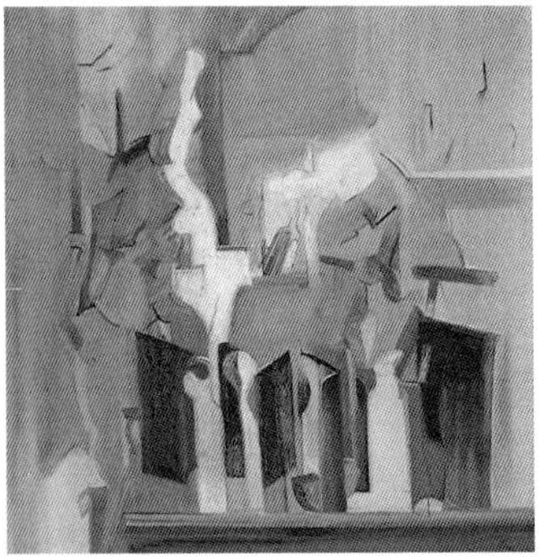

66

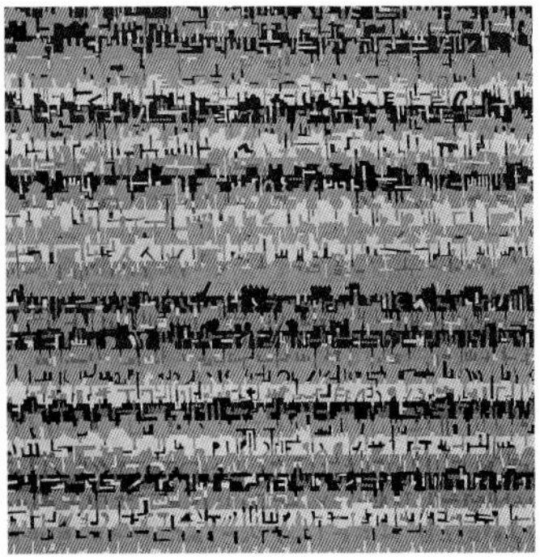

67

WILLIAM TURNBULL b.1922

68 **Head** 1955

Inscribed b.r.: 'Turnbull 55'
Oil on paper 71.3 × 52.1 cm
Purchased: Waddington Galleries, December 1985

69 **Headform** 1956

Inscribed b.l.: '24/30' and b.r.: 'Turnbull 56'
Serigraph in black and blue 76.5 × 56 cm (paper size)
Edition of 30
Purchased: The artist 1986

Turnbull was born in Dundee in 1922. Like his fellow Scot Paolozzi, he was at the Slade in London from 1946 to 1948 and then lived in Paris until 1950, when he returned to London to exhibit at the Hanover Gallery. Giacometti's influence is evident in the attenuated structures of plaster on metal armatures which Turnbull showed then and at Venice in the Biennale of 1952. He, Paolozzi and their mutual friend Nigel Henderson were all fascinated by the human head. Relevant here is an exhibition at the Institute of Contemporary Arts in March 1953, *Wonder and Horror of the Human Head*, though their interest predates this and can be related to the works of the Dadaists, Klee, tribal sculptors, Picasso and others they saw in Paris. One of the things that interested them was how immediately recognizable the human head was, even though the image was far removed from 'reality'.

William Turnbull, Sculpture and Painting, Tate Gallery 1973
P. Gilmour, *The Mechanised Image : A Historical Perspective of 20th Century Prints*, Arts Council of Great Britain 1978
The Independent Group : Postwar Britain and the Aesthetics of Plenty, Institute of Contemporary Arts, London 1990

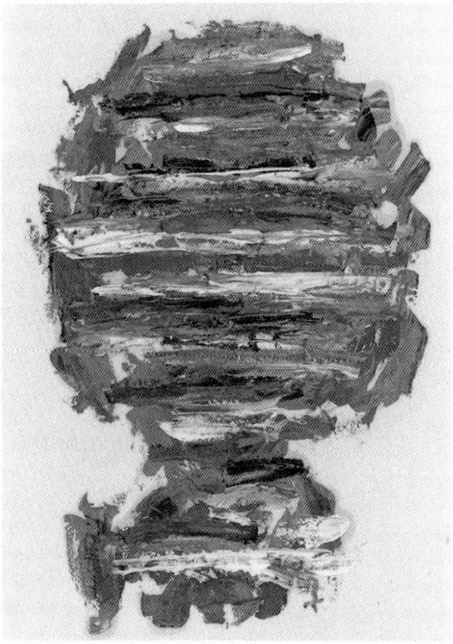

68

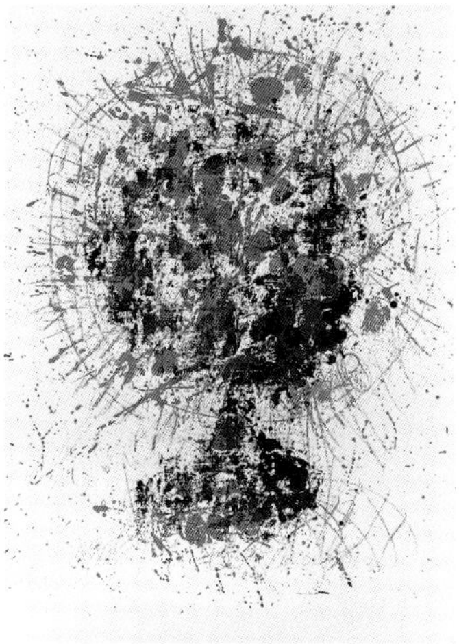

69

JOHN WELLS b.1907

70 **Untitled** 1958

Inscribed b.l.: 'John Wells. 1958'
Lithograph 50.8 × 65 cm (paper size)
Artist's proof printed by Stanley Jones in St. Ives apart from the edition of 30
Purchased: New Art Centre, London 1986

Wells qualified as a doctor in 1930 and practised in the Scilly Isles from 1936-45 when he moved to Newlyn. He co-founded the Crypt Group in St. Ives in 1946 and the Penwith Society in 1949. He has enjoyed the friendship of Ben Nicholson, Barbara Hepworth, Alexander Mackenzie and Denis Mitchell.

St. Ives 1939-64, Tate Gallery 1985

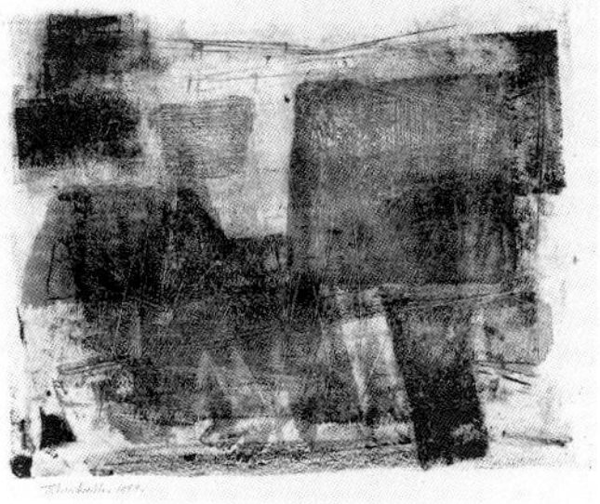

70

GILLIAN WISE b.1936

71 **Brown and Orange Relief with Prisms** 1960

Inscribed on reverse: 'Gillian Wise/BROWN AND ORANGE RELIEF WITH PRISMS/1960'
Wood, plastic, perspex and glass 37.6 × 61 cm
Exhibited: *Anthony Hill/Gillian Wise*, Institute of Contemporary Arts, London February 1963, no. 15; *Construction England*, Arts Council touring exhibition 1963, no. 49
Purchased: Annely Juda Fine Art, London 1974

72 **Metal Relief with Horizontal Elements** 1962

Inscribed on reverse: 'RELIEF WITH HORIZONTAL ELEMENTS/1962 ANTHONY HILL GILLIAN WISE'
Aluminium, tin and perspex 45.2 × 64.7 cm
Exhibited: *Anthony Hill/Gillian Wise*, Institute of Contemporary Arts February 1963, no. 25 (reproduced on cover)
Purchased: Anthony Hill 1974-5
This work was executed jointly with Anthony Hill

Gillian Wise studied at Wimbledon Art School from 1954-7. She exchanged letters with the American constructionist Charles Biederman and through him met Anthony Hill in 1958. They shared an exhibition of constructed reliefs at the Institute of Contemporary Arts in 1963 where both the reliefs in Powell's collection were shown. No.72 is in fact a joint work made with Anthony Hill. Wise brought to relief-making a concern with reflecting surfaces and colour. From Vantongerloo she derived the idea of using glass prisms to reflect light brightly into the core of her work and most of her reliefs shown at the Institute of Contemporary Arts in 1963 incorporate prisms.

She went on to develop a series of reliefs and shallow boxes with planes of transparent perspex, linked by elastic thread, inspired by the mathematician Guiseppe Peano. These were shown in a one-person exhibition at the Polytechnic of Central London in 1975. She has participated in many group shows including *Construction : England 1950-60* at the Drian Gallery, 1961; *Systeemi-System* at the Amos Anderson Taidemuseo, Helsinki, 1969; *Systems*, Arts Council of Great Britain, 1972; and the Hayward Annual, 1978. She lives and works in Paris.

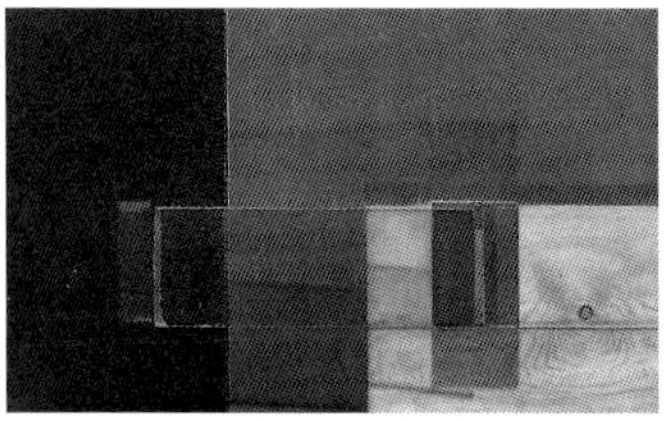

71

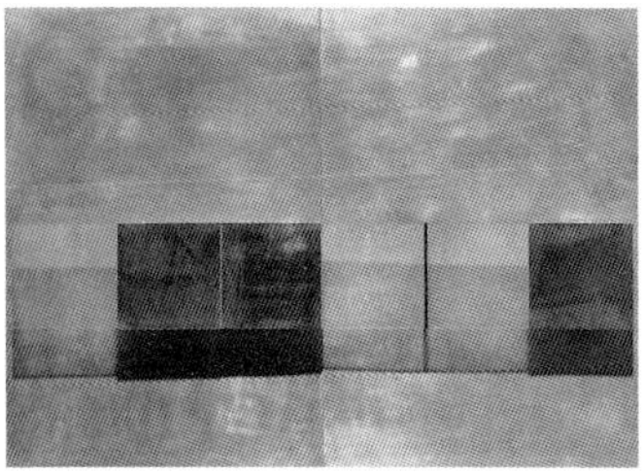

72

A. Hill (ed.), *DATA, Directions in Art, Theory and Aesthetics*, London 1968
Constructive Context, An exhibition selected from the Arts Council Collection by Stephen Bann, Arts Council of Great Britain 1978
And the catalogues of the exhibitions listed above

chronology of important events + exhibitions **1945–1962**

For artists' individual exhibitions, see the catalogue entries.
This chronology is a revised version of one published by Alastair Grieve for the conference *Rational Practice* at the Gardner Centre, University of Sussex, 1978.

1945 Arts Council of Great Britain established.

December, *Picasso* and *Matisse* exhibitions, Victoria and Albert Museum.

1946 Gimpel Fils Gallery established in London.

Braque and *Rouault* exhibitions at re-opened Tate Gallery.

Salon des Réalités Nouvelles founded, Paris.

1948 Institute of Contemporary Arts founded in London. First exhibition, 9 February-6 March, *40 Years of Modern Art 1907-1947*, Academy Hall, Oxford Street.

May-June, London Group exhibition. Abstract artists showed regularly in subsequent exhibitions, not listed here.

May-September, first London County Council *Sculpture in the Open Air* exhibition.

30 November-31 December, *Colour Prints by Society of London Painter Printers*, Redfern Gallery, London. Abstract artists showed prints in subsequent exhibitions not listed here.

20 December-29 January (1949), *40,000 Years of Modern Art* I.C.A., Academy Hall.

1949 Penwith Society founded in St. Ives.

February, entire Tate Gallery re-opens.

1950 March-April, *London-Paris*, I.C.A., New Burlington Galleries, London.

13 December-12 January (1951), *Aspects of British Art*, I.C.A. opening exhibition at Dover Street premises in London.

1951 January, *Calder* exhibition, Lefevre Gallery, London.

January-March, *L'École de Paris*, Royal Academy.

May, *60 Paintings for '51*, Arts Council touring exhibition of large paintings opens at Manchester City Art Gallery.

May-September, *Festival of Britain*, South Bank, London.

22 May-11 June, *Abstract Painting, Sculptures, Mobiles*, A.I.A. Gallery, Lisle Street, London.

4 July-31 August, *Growth and Form*, I.C.A.

August, *British Abstract Art*, Gimpel Fils Gallery.

October, *Le Groupe Espace* founded in Paris.

1952 21 February-15 March, *de Staël* exhibition, Matthiesen Gallery, London.

21-23 March, first *Abstract Art* exhibition 22 Fitzroy Street, London.

1952 Spring, *Fifty Years of Dutch Painting* (including *De Stijl*) Redfern Gallery.

14 June-19 October, *New Aspects of British Sculpture*, XXVI Biennale, Venice.

15 July-17 August, *XXth Century Masterpieces*, Tate Gallery.

11-14 July, second *Abstract Art* exhibition, 22 Fitzroy Street.

2-20 December, *The Mirror and the Square*, A.I.A., New Burlington Galleries.

1953 28 January -28 February, *Opposing Forces*, (*Tachiste* and Abstract Expressionist), I.C.A.

March, *Wonder and Horror of the Human Head*, I.C.A.

14 March-30 April, *The Unknown Political Prisoner, International Sculpture Competition*, Tate Gallery.

April-May, *Le Corbusier* exhibition, I.C.A.

1-4 May, third *Abstract Art* exhibition, 22 Fitzroy Street.

7 July-7 August, *Space in Colour*, Hanover Gallery, London.

10 September-18 October, *Parallel of Life and Art*, I.C.A.

November-December, Curt Valentin's *Collection of Drawings by Paul Klee*, I.CA.

1954 13 April-8 May, *Cubism, Abstractionism, Sur-Realism, Formalism*, Redfern Gallery.

19 May-9 June, *Artist v. Machine*, Building Centre, Store Street, London.

13 October-20 November, *Collages and Objects*, I.C.A.

25 October-27 November, *Romantic Abstraction*, Symon Quinn Gallery, Huddersfield.

November, publication of L. Alloway, *Nine Abstract Artists* London (Tiranti).

1955 11-29 January, *Nine Abstract Artists* exhibition, Redfern Gallery.

6-30 April, *Le Mouvement* exhibition, Galerie Denise René, Paris.

10-29 May, *Measurement and Proportion*, A.I.A. Gallery, Lisle Street.

May, *Abstract Painting from Paris*, Symon Quinn Gallery, Huddersfield.

May, *Man, Machine and Motion*, Hatton Gallery, Newcastle-upon-Tyne.

August-September, *Mondrian* exhibition, Whitechapel Art Gallery, London.

1956 2-27 January, *Aspects of Contemporary English Painting*, Parsons Gallery, London.

5 January-12 February, *Modern Art in the United States*, Tate Gallery.

May, *de Staël* exhibition, Whitechapel Art Gallery.

2-16 June, *Abstracts*, Hatton Gallery, Newcastle-upon-Tyne.

Realist artists from Beaux Arts Gallery in British section at Venice Biennale.

July-September, *Contemporary Sculpture*, Hanover Gallery.

1956 9 August-9 September, *This is Tomorrow*, Whitechapel Art Gallery.

1956 3-20 December, *Recent Abstract Painting*, Whitworth Art Gallery, Manchester.

1957 16 January-16 February, *Statements – A Review of British Abstract Art in 1956*, I.C.A.

4 April-4 May, *Metavisual Tachiste Abstract, Painting in England Today*, Redfern Gallery.

6-26 May, *Abstract*, A.I.A. Gallery.

June, *An Exhibit*, Hatton Gallery, Newcastle-upon-Tyne.

23 July-1 September, *Living Art*, Lords Gallery, London.

6-30 November, *Pictures without Paint*, A.I.A. Gallery.

6-21 December, *Dimensions, British Abstract Art 1948-57*, O'Hana Gallery, London.

Foundation of Zero Group, Düsseldorf.

1958 March, *Some Paintings from the E.J. Power Collection*, I.C.A.

28 March-23 April, *25th Anniversary Exhibition of A.I.A.*, R.B.A. Galleries, Suffolk Street, London.

November, *Pollock* exhibition, Whitechapel Art Gallery.

Structure, Annual on the New Art, launched by Joost Baljeu and Eli Bornstein.

1959 24 February-22 March, *The New American Painting*, Tate Gallery.

April-May, *The Developing Process*, I.C.A.

6 August-6 September, *Paintings, Drawings, Reliefs*, A.I.A. Gallery.

October-November, *Malevich* exhibition, Whitechapel Art Gallery.

1960 *The Structurist*, ed. Eli Bornstein, launched.

8 June-14 August, *Konkrete Kunst*, Helmhaus, Zurich.

September, *Situation : an Exhibition of British Abstract Painting*, R.B.A. Galleries.

G.R.A.V. founded in Paris.

1961 11 January-4 February, *Construction : England :1950-60*, Drian Galleries, Porchester Place, London.

20 June-12 July, *Directions, Connections : Architecture, Painting, Sculpture*, A.I.A. Gallery.

3-7 July, *Sixth Congress of the International Union of Architects*, South Bank.

October, *British Constructivist Art*, exhibition organized by the I.C.A. begins tour of U.S.A.

New Tendency founded, Zagreb.

1962 10-31 May, *The Geometric Environment*, A.I.A. Gallery.

18 May-16 June, *Experiment in Constructie*, Stedelijk Museum, Amsterdam.

Constructivisme, Galerie Dautzenberg, Paris.

October-November, *Kompas 2*, Stedelijk Van Abbemuseum, Eindhoven.

bibliography

Some books and articles which were important in the formation of constructed abstract art c.1950:

H. Arp, *On My Way*, New York (Wittenborn) 1948

C. Biederman, *Art as the Evolution of Visual Knowedge*, Red Wing 1948

C. Biederman, *Letters on the New Art*, Red Wing 1951

A. Collingridge, 'The Golden Section', *Eidos, Journal of Painting, Sculpture and Design* no.2, September-October 1950, p.43

T. A. Cook, *The Curves of Life*, London 1914

Le Corbusier, *The Modulor*, Paris 1950

G. Diehl, *Les Problèmes de la Peinture* (Jacques Villon on construction and colour), Paris 1945

M. Ghyka, *The Geometry of Art and Life*, New York 1946

M. Ghyka, 'Le Corbusier's Modulor', *Architectural Review*, February 1948, pp.39-42

J. Hambidge, *Dynamic Symmetry in Composition*, New Haven 1923, reprint 1948

J. Hambidge, *The Elements of Dynamic Symmetry*, New Haven 1919, 1920, reprint 1948

D. H. Kahnweiler, *Juan Gris*, London 1947

P. Klee, *On Modern Art*, London (Faber) 1948

P. Mondrian, *Plastic Art and Pure Plastic Art*, New York (Wittenborn) 1945

J. W. Power, *Les Éléments de la Construction Picturale*, Paris 1933

M. Seuphor, *L'Art Abstrait*, Paris 1949

D'Arcy Wentworth Thompson, *On Growth and Form*, Cambridge 1942

G. Vantongerloo, *Paintings, Sculptures, Reflections*, New York (Wittenborn) 1948

R. Wittkower, *Architectural Principles in the Age of Humanism*, London 1949

Books, articles and catalogues on British Art in the 1950s relevant to the artists in Ken Powell's collection (for individual artists, see the catalogue entries)

L. Alloway (ed), *Nine Abstract Artists*, London (Tiranti) 1954

F. Carey and A. Griffiths, *Avant-Garde British Printmaking 1914-1960*, The Trustees of the British Museum 1990

Corsham, A Celebration, the Bath Academy of Art 1946-72, Victoria Art Gallery, Bath 1988

The Forgotten Fifties, Graves Art Gallery, Sheffield 1984

A. I. Grieve, 'Towards an art of environment: exhibitions and publications by a group of avant-garde abstract artists in London 1951-55' *The Burlington Magazine* CXXXII, no.1052, November 1990, pp.773-781

A. Hill (ed.), *DATA, Directions in Art, Theory and Aesthetics*, London 1968

The Independent Group : Postwar Britain and the Aesthetics of Plenty, Institute of Contemporary Arts, London 1990

A. Lewis, 'British Avant-Garde Painting I, II, III', *Artscribe* nos. 34,35,36, March, June, August 1982, pp.16-54, 16-31, 14-27

S. Nairne and N. Serota, (eds) *British Sculpture in the Twentieth Century*, Whitechapel Art Gallery, London 1981

St. Ives 1939-64, Twenty Five Years of Painting, Sculpture and Pottery, The Tate Gallery 1985

A Selection of Postwar British Abstract Art, introduction by Margaret Garlake, Austin / Desmond Fine Art, London 1988